SAMURAI WARLORDS

Hajikano leads the Takeda army to Odawara

This plate reproduces a dramatic moment during the Takeda army's advance against the Hōjō family in 1569. As the army under Takeda Shingen (shown here wearing a red *jinbaori* surcoat) moved against the Hōjō's fortress of Odawara, their progress was halted by the swollen waters of the Sasaogawa river. One of Shingen's junior commanders, Hajikano Masatsugu, who bore the rank of *ashigaru-taishō* (general of foot-soldiers), volunteered for the dangerous task of assessing the depth of the raging river. He rode his horse into the water and, having first tested the depth with the shaft of his spear, rode on until for a brief moment only the *sashimono* flag on the back of his armour was visible above the surface. The design on the banner was one of the playing pieces in the Japanese board game of *shōgi*, representing a spear, which in *shōgi* can only move forward, and not retreat. Hajikano put this to Shingen as a reason for his confidence in advancing.

Hajikano Masatsugu is drawn according to his description in the account of the incident in the *Kōyō Gunkan*. The flags among the Takeda army are those of the two subordinate commanders who attended Shingen on this occasion, Naitō Masatoyo and Baba Nobuharu.

STEPHEN TURNBULL

SAMURAI WARLORDS

The Book of the Daimyō

Illustrated by James Field

BLANDFORD

This paperback edition 1992
First published in the UK 1989 by Blandford,
an imprint of Cassell
Villiers House, 41/47 Strand,
London, WC2N 5JE

Copyright © Blandford Press 1989
Text copyright © Stephen Turnbull 1989
Colour artwork © James Field 1989

CIP data is available upon request from
the British Library National Bibliographic Service

Distributed in the United States by
Sterling Publishing Co., Inc.,
387 Park Avenue South,
New York, NY 10016-8810

Distributed in Australia by
Capricorn Link (Australia) Pty Ltd,
PO Box 665, Lane Cove, NSW 2066

ISBN 0 7137 20034 hardback
ISBN 0 7137 23297 paperback

Printed and bound in
Singapore by Kyodo
Printing Industries PTE Ltd.

To Katy Turnbull

Contents

Introduction

The samurai were the military élite of old Japan, and the daimyō, the 'Samurai Warlords', were the élite of the samurai. This book is therefore about the *'crème de la crème'* of the samurai class — the samurai who succeeded first as warriors, and went on to found petty kingdoms of their own, which they defended with armies of samurai who owed allegiance to them and to none other. From these original warlords grew great dynasties of daimyō, who enjoyed a symbiotic existence with the central government of the Shōgun until all were swept away in the upheavals of the 1850s which gave birth to modern Japan.

There is a popular theory, nowadays, that one reason the Japanese are so successful in the modern world is that they give to their company, and to their country, that same loyalty which once they gave to the daimyō. In the pages that follow we shall see of what that fierce loyalty consisted.

Unlike any of the present author's previous books on the samurai, this work is not arranged chronologically, but as a series of chapters, each of which examines in depth a particular role which the daimyō was required to play. We shall see him as a warrior, as a commander and as a focus for that legendary loyalty which still amazes one even today. We shall examine his other demanding duties as the founder of a dynasty, as the keeper of the peace and as the patron of the arts. To be a daimyō was a demanding life, and the demands did not stop with the warlord's death, for he then entered on a new and strange role as spiritual guardian of the family, to be honoured, and, if necessary, bloodily revenged.

In a sense, this book is about two very different types of people, the *sengoku-daimyō*, the warlords of the Sengoku Period, or the 'Age of War' (which is roughly the same as the sixteenth century AD), and the daimyō of the Edo Period, the three centuries that followed, which were marked by the almost total absence of war. The lives of these two groups were very different but closely related, because it was the experience of life in the Age of War, or at the very least the tradition passed on from their ancestors, that prepared the later daimyō to survive the different demands of the Age of Peace. It is this thread of tradition of self-sacrifice, of the needs of the group, of identification with a leader, that tells us so much about Japan today.

This book is based entirely upon Japanese sources, and therefore could not have been written without the help and support of many people. First mention, as ever, must go to Mrs Nahoko Kitajima for her assistance, especially during the preparation for my study tour in 1986. I would like to thank the staff of the Oriental Collections at the British Library, particularly Mrs Yu-Ying Brown, for guiding me through the valuable source materials I have used here. Once again it has been a pleasure to work with James Field, and to see my ideas and notes translated into his splendid paintings. The colour photographs are all my own, but I would like to thank several people for allowing me to photograph the black-and-white material that

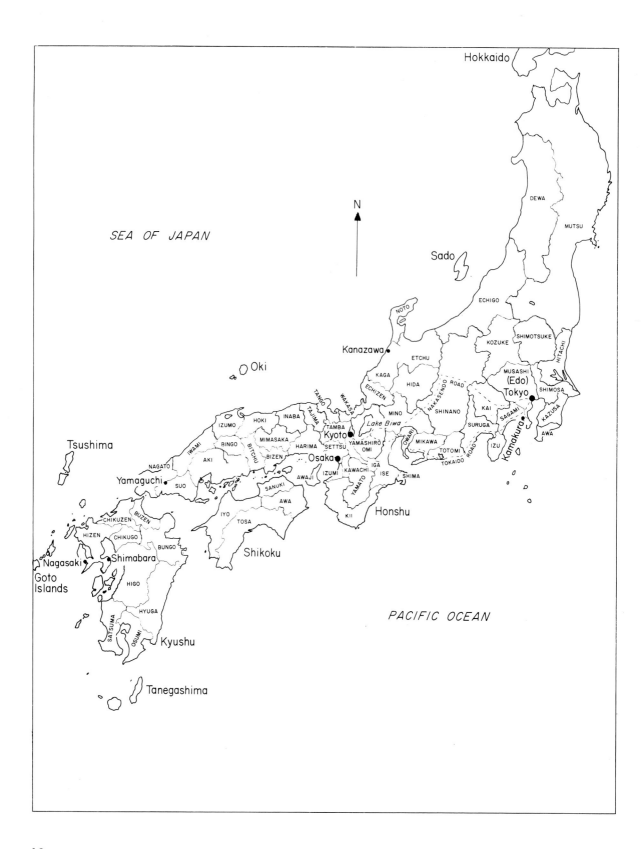

has provided the fine detail of the past. In particular, I am indebted to Dunstan Gladthorpe for supplying photographs from the pages of his copies of the *Hōjō Godai-ki* and the *Ehon Taikō-ki*.

My greatest thanks are, of course, to my dear wife Jo, and my three *wakamusha*, Alex, Richard and Katy. They have now endured nine books, and without them, nothing would happen.

Stephen Turnbull
Leeds 1988

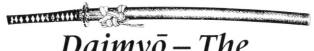

Daimyō – The Warlords of Japan

Hōjō Sōun leads his followers into Izu

Hōjō Sōun's most decisive move was his invasion of Izu, an operation nominally carried out to avenge the murder of the former *shugo* of the province. It resulted in the allegiance to Sōun of the former retainers of Izu, and Sōun's establishment as a daimyō. In this illustration, taken from an eighteenth-century wood-block-printed edition of the *Hōjō Godai-ki*, Sōun used his war-fan to signal to his men in a charge. One of his samurai lunges at an enemy with a barbed rake.

In 1491 a 60-year-old samurai, who, the chronicles tell us, had 'clear eyesight, good hearing and all his own teeth', invaded the province of Izu and started a revolution.

The man's name was Ise Shinkuro Nagauji, better known to posterity as Hōjō Sōun, and known to the eastern provinces as the first 'Samurai Warlord'. The eventual success of his conquests, and his ability to control them and pass them on to his descendants, marked him out as a new breed of samurai leader, and he was to become famous for his military skill, his political cunning, and his religious faith. He was also to become legendary for his longevity. He was certainly no wild young samurai warrior when he invaded Izu, and he still had another 27 years of active life ahead of him.

Hōjō Sōun called himself a *daimyō*, a word which, when literally trans-

lated means 'great name'. 'Warlord' is an English word which conveniently encompasses in its associations everything that made the daimyō what they were. The revolution Hōjō Sōun caused in Izu, which gave him the territory for his own, brought to that particular area of Japan the notion of *gekokujō*, 'the low overcome the high', the savage principle of opportunistic rebellion sweeping away the old order, which was to characterise sixteenth-century Japan, and set the pattern whereby other 'great names' could be made in other parts of Japan, until by the third quarter of the sixteenth century these daimyō warlords controlled huge territories as independent princes.

The Hōjō family, whom we shall examine in some detail in this chapter, are prime examples of the daimyō of the Sengoku Period, the 'Age of War', which is roughly coterminous with the sixteenth century AD. In the chapters which follow, we shall note various aspects of the role of the daimyō of the 'Age of War', and compare them with those of the 'Age of Peace' which followed.

The rise of the samurai

The part of Japan where the Hōjō established themselves was known as the Kantō, a word which means 'east of the barrier'. The barrier in question was an ancient toll-barrier in the Hakone Mountains, although the mountains themselves were as secure and forbidding a barrier as any that the hand of man could provide. The deeply wooded Hakone Mountains, which

The Hakone Mountains
The proud Hōjō family, the archetypal daimyō of the Sengoku Period, relied as much on the natural defences provided by the Hakone Mountains as on their numerous castles. This view is taken looking across terraced rice fields at the time of the transplanting of rice seedlings in May.

The Samurai

The samurai were the élite of old Japan, and the daimyō were the élite of the samurai. This actor from the Toei-Uzumasa Film Studios in Kyōto is dressed in the costume of the samurai retainer of a daimyō of the Edo Period, with the characteristic two swords. He wears a loose jacket, called a *haori*, and on his feet are wooden *geta*.

are foothills to the crowning glory of the gigantic Mount Fuji, provided an obstacle to east–west communications until the present century, allowing the inhabitants of the fertile Kantō plain, with its ready access to the sea, to develop relatively unhindered by political and military changes in the more sophisticated western provinces. Civilisation came from the west, from the capital city of Nara, until AD 794 when it was replaced by Kyōto, also in the west.

The Kantō, by contrast, bred warriors. From the Kantō had come the samurai warriors of the Minamoto clan in the twelfth century, who had fought the western Taira clan in a fierce civil war from 1180 to 1185, which had ended with the Taira destroyed in a naval battle so bloody that the seas had turned red. The Taira had ruled from Kyōto, marrying successive daughters into the imperial family and making their own family the dominant line of government. The victorious Minamoto needed no political chicanery. It was military force that had put them in a position of power, so it was by military force that they would rule. The Emperor was condemned to being a shadowy living god. Real power lay with the possessor of the title of *Shōgun* which the Minamoto leader was granted by the powerless Emperor – 'commander-in-chief for the suppression of barbarians'.

The first Shōgun, Minamoto Yoritomo, chose to base himself at Kamakura, in the heart of the Kantō, past the barrier and far from Kyōto. But even the mighty Minamoto were not to last forever, and in 1333 the old imperial capital became also the Shōgun's capital when the founder of a new dynasty, the Ashikaga, moved his seat of government westwards. The Ashikaga dynasty, too, began its own curve of triumph and decline, frustrated by the problems of controlling a disparate country where communications were difficult and centuries of warfare had bred distrust and resilience among their subjects.

The Ashikaga Shōgun's rule in the provinces was devolved through men called the *shugo* and the *jitō*. The *jitō* were the civil arm of local government, and the *shugo* the military. The Nambokuchō civil wars of 1330 to 1392 greatly weakened the authority of the *jitō* until, by the beginning of the fifteenth century, the *shugo* stood alone as the Shōgun's deputy and military governor. Many were related by blood to the Ashikaga. Others were appointed for no better reason than that they were the strongest samurai in the province and thus more likely to command respect. It was useful for the Ashikaga Shōgun to have someone they could rely on, and gradually the *shugo* acquired more devolved powers.

The centre collapses

As long as the Ashikaga stayed in control there was no problem of stability, and when the fifteenth century began the Ashikaga were at the height of their powers. Ashikaga Yoshimitsu had built a pavilion coated with gold, and had entertained princes and ambassadors, and now his successors looked as if they would lift the dynasty to greater heights. Then one by one, the blows came. In 1441 the sixth Ashikaga Shōgun, Yoshinori, was murdered. He was succeeded by an 8-year-old son, who died two years later, to be followed by his younger brother Yoshimasa. Yoshimasa, in fact, reigned as Shōgun for 30 years, and witnessed the gradual seeping away of all Shōgunal authority. Power passed into the hands of the *shugo*; but theirs

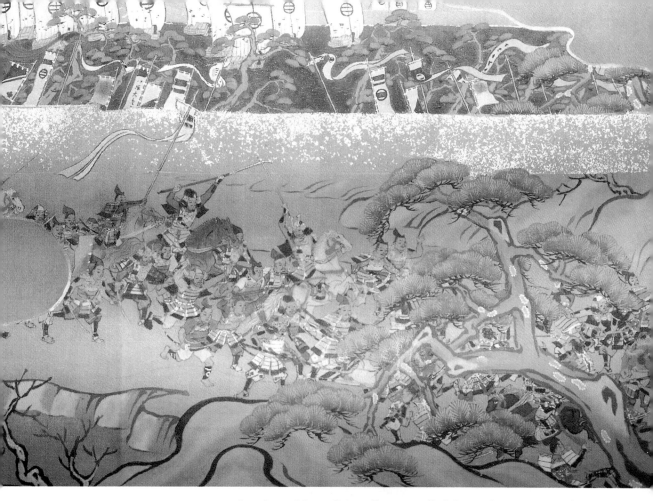

The Battle of Minatogawa
This section of a painted scroll at the Nampian Kannon-ji at Kawachi-Nagano (reproduced here by kind permission of the Chief Priest) depicts the last battle fought by the hero, Kusunoki Masashige. In the background, troops of the Hosokawa clan are landed from boats, an action which cut Kusunoki off from assistance, and led to his death by suicide. It was the defeat of the Kusunoki that paved the way for the establishment of the Ashikaga dynasty of Shōguns.

was an ordered world, traditionally controlled from the centre, and the centre, in the shape of Kyōto and the artistic and sensitive Shōgun, kept pulling them in. So they clung to Kyōto, to their mansions and their gardens, and to the Ashikaga grandees who made a great show of 'carrying on as normal'. Meanwhile their own authority in the provinces began to slip away, until in 1467, in an act of reckless disregard for political reality, the *shugo* once more gathered in Kyōto, but this time it was to fight a war amongst their own kind.

The Ōnin War, which had Kyōto as its first battlefield, dragged on for ten years, during which the fighting spread to the provinces and the *shugo* families fought each other to extinction. Others rushed to fill the gaps their deaths had caused, persons who knew nothing of the Shōgun's commissions and poetry parties in Kyōto. These 'new men' were peasant farmers, or oil sellers, or blacksmiths, men who realised that only military force was now needed. They would gather round them a handful of like-minded souls who were good fighters, and build a secure stockade on a hill, from where they could defend their rice fields. No tax-collector would be coming from Kyōto. No message would arrive from the Shōgun requesting them to chastise rebels on his behalf. Now was the time to build one's own kingdom and make a name for oneself, to make oneself a 'big name' – a daimyō.

That was where most of the daimyō came from. Some *shugo* families did

17

survive and themselves became daimyō, but they tended either to be remote from Kyōto, or to have received the commission of *shugo* as an act of desperation on the part of the Shōgun. In the majority of cases, daimyō were created by *gekokujō*-style usurpation. Existing *shugo* were murdered by their subjects. Brothers, fathers even, were deposed. Daughters were traded like horses to secure alliances, as the territories grew from one hill-top fortress to two, then three, surrounding a fertile valley. Then a neighbour's lands were seized, and the area doubled, and so it grew. The map of Japan began to resemble the playing-board for a game of *go*, where the protagonists begin with an empty board. One by one spaces are surrounded and captured, then themselves are swallowed within another growing territory, until at the end of the game there are no spaces left to occupy, and there is only one winner.

Hōjō – the exemplary daimyō

The end of the game was over a century away when Hōjō Sōun led his samurai into Izu. Over the next four generations of the family, the Hōjō illustrated all of the aspects of daimyō rule which are discussed in the following chapters, the foremost of which was the ability to wage war.

The first point to note about the Hōjō was their comparatively humble origin. The Hōjō did not originate in the Kantō. Hōjō Sōun was very probably the son of a minor official of the Ashikaga Shōgun, based in Kyōto. He was born in 1432 and was educated by the monks of the Daitoku-ji, and was therefore 35 years old when the old capital was torn apart by the long and terrible Ōnin War. Sōun managed to leave Kyōto and the devastation the Ōnin War had caused sometime around 1469. He had with him a band of six loyal samurai, and took up a position with Imagawa Yoshitada, who had married Sōun's sister, and held the post of *shugo* of Suruga province. In 1476 Imagawa Yoshitada was killed in battle, and a succession dispute arose among the Imagawa retainers. Sōun, who was perceived as a well-educated and disinterested party, acted as chief mediator between the factions, and secured the succession for his nephew, Imagawa Ujichika. The grateful Ujichika rewarded his uncle with the castle of Kōkokuji, and Sōun's band of loyal samurai started to grow.

The need to build a retainer band was a vital characteristic of the daimyō. The small band of followers which Sōun had brought with him from Kyōto grew into an army as Sōun developed the means to feed them, and the success to attract them to him. These were the men he led into Izu, the most important turning-point in his career. It is also a classic illustration of *gekokujō*. Sooner or later every successful daimyō had to strike, and strike hard to establish himself as somehow superior to the competition, and to intervene in a succession dispute in a neighbouring family was an ideal technique. The *shugo* of Izu was of the Ashikaga family, one Masatomo, and when he died his son, known only by his boy's name of Chachamaru, succeeded to the post by murdering his mother and his elder brother. The old retainers of Izu were horrified at the act and turned against him. Hōjō Sōun, watching from the neighbouring province, resolved to avenge the father. He crossed the provincial border and attacked, forcing the treacherous Chachamaru to commit suicide. All the retainers of the former *shugo* gladly submitted to the honourable Sōun, and by their acclamation Izu was his.

Odawara castle
Odawara castle became the capital of the Hōjō territories when it was captured by Hōjō Sōun in 1518, and stayed in their possession until 1590, in spite of numerous attacks by the Takeda and the Uesugi. The present keep is a modern reconstruction.

Sōun had therefore moved on from the ownership of one castle, given by the Imagawa, to controlling a whole province, with no grant from a Shōgun, or commission from the emperor. It is about this time that he changed his name to Hōjō. There had been a famous Hōjō family centuries before. Sōun had no connection with them, of course, but the name had a certain ring to it, and in the climate that was developing in Japan at the time, surnames, like provinces, were there for the taking.

Four years later, he cast his eyes eastwards along the sea coast and sided with one of the quarrelsome branches of the doomed Uesugi family. This further piece of opportunism won him the strategic castle of Odawara, soon to become the Hōjō capital, and gave him a secure base in western Sagami. In 1512 he captured the old Shōgunal capital of Kamakura, and then completed the conquest of Sagami province in 1518 with the defeat

Building a Castle

This scene represents the building of a castle round about the year 1600. Two officials examine the plans, while a surveyor checks the line of building. In the background a final stone is levered into place around the massive earth core, while the wooden beams that will form the skeleton of the keep begin to take on the shape of the finished building.

The building of castles was one of the most important steps in establishing the *daimyō* of the Sengoku Period as the most important powers in their particular areas. Whereas earlier castles had been fortresses made of wood and earth that clung to the natural topography of mountains, or were concealed among meandering watercourses, the new castles had all their defences built in to their design, and much stone was used in their construction. Their location was chosen on the basis of the control it offered over lines of communication through their provinces, regardless of any natural defensive aspect. Toyotomi Hideyoshi appreciated the power of a large and well-garrisoned castle, and took steps to restrict their proliferation among potential rivals. Castle-building was further controlled under the Tokugawa.

Many of the Japanese castles that have survived to this day, such as Himeji and Hikone, were started during the Sengoku Period.

of the Miura family at Arai in 1518 – a battle famous for the defiant act of suicide by the Miura family's heir, who is supposed to have cut his own head off.

Ujitsuna and Ujiyasu carry the flag

The following year Hōjō Sōun died at the age of 87, a man who had sprung from nowhere, who had witnessed the Ōnin War and its destruction of the *shugo*, and had gone on to become daimyō of two provinces. He had, in fact, retired from the position of daimyō the previous year to allow his son Ujitsuna to begin his rule while he still had his father to help him. The succession of a series of eldest sons was one of the Hōjō dynasty's great strengths, which stands in marked contrast to the unhappy experience of

Hōjō Ujitsuna
Ujitsuna was Sōun's son and heir, and continued the process of conquest of the Kantō which his father had begun. He defeated the Uesugi at Edo, the Satomi at Kōnodai, and established the temple of Sōun-ji in his father's memory.

other families we shall discuss in a later chapter. Although less colourful a character than his father, Ujitsuna was to continue the process of conquest and consolidation that Sōun had begun.

The vital factor in the continuity of the operation was the loyalty of the family retainers. Soon after his father's death, Ujitsuna founded the temple of Sōun-ji in Sōun's memory, which impressed the old retainers considerably, and they showed their faith in Sōun's heir by fighting valiantly for him when he expanded the Hōjō domain further into the Kantō by defeating the Uesugi at their castle of Edo in 1524. This village at the mouth of the Sumida River, which is now the city of Tōkyō, was the key to Musashi province, which Ujitsuna confirmed by defeating the combined forces of Satomi Yoshitaka and Ashikaga Yoshiaki at the Battle of Kōnodai in 1538.

To some extent, Ujitsuna had a much more difficult task than his father. Sōun, admittedly, had had the uphill job of establishing himself from nowhere; but by the time Ujitsuna was in command, there was much less opportunity for *gekokujō*. Ujitsuna's enemies were daimyō like himself, not decaying *shugo*. Apart from the odd opportunistic assassination and the dubious activities of *ninja*, issues had to be settled by warfare. Ujitsuna, therefore, concentrated heavily on building up his army, and establishing an efficient system of military obligation, which is discussed in detail in the following chapter. He also established laws, and made sure that within the Hōjō domain it was Hōjō law that mattered. But the daimyō was still first and foremost a military leader, and Ujitsuna saw it as his duty to lead his samurai personally into battle.

The Sōun-ji
It was vitally important for Hōjō Ujitsuna to retain the loyal service of his late father's old followers, and one way in which he did it was to found this temple, the Sōun-ji, at Yumoto, near Odawara. It lies at the foot of the Hakone Mountains, on the course of the old Tōkaidō road, and has recently been re-roofed.

Like his father before him, Ujitsuna groomed his son Ujiyasu for his eventual succession. Also like Sōun, Ujitsuna left behind a set of House Laws to guide future generations. In one section he warns: 'After winning a great victory, a haughty heart, disdain for the enemy, and incautious actions often follow. Avoid this. There have been many families in the past destroyed in this manner.'

Ujitsuna died in 1541. The third daimyō, Hōjō Ujiyasu, continued the conquests of his predecessors until, by 1560, when he retired in favour of his son Ujimasa, the Hōjō controlled most of the Kantō region.

Ujiyasu was Sōun reborn. To defend the Kantō from the north, his father had established a series of forts along the Sumidagawa, and in defending one of these, Kawagoe, Ujiyasu won his most celebrated victory in 1545. The Battle of Kawagoe has a special place in samurai history in that it was fought at night, which alone pays tribute to Ujiyasu's skills in handling troops. In 1564 Ujiyasu again demonstrated his skills as a general in a remarkable 're-run' of his father's battle at Kōnodai in 1538. In the second Battle of Kōnodai, Hōjō Ujiyasu, son of the previous victor, defeated Satomi Yoshihiro, son of the daimyō formerly vanquished.

Hōjō Ujiyasu
Hōjō Ujiyasu (1515–70) was the grandson of the founder of the family, Hōjō Sōun, and the descendant most like his illustrious predecessor. He led the celebrated night attack on the besieging forces of the Uesugi at Kawagoe in 1545, which was held for the Hōjō by his adopted brother Hōjō Tsunanari, and won the second Battle of Kōnodai in 1564. It was Ujiyasu who led the family to its greatest heights of achievement, in spite of competition from other powerful daimyō, such as Takeda Shingen.

The second Battle of Kōnodai (1564)
Kōnodai, on the edge of what is now Tōkyō Bay, saw two battles between two generations of the Hōjō family and the Satomi. In both, the Hōjō were victorious. In this vigorous illustration from the *Hōjō Godai-ki*, the Hōjō samurai use their swords and spear to deadly effect against the Satomi soldiers.

The territories meet

At this point a new dimension entered into the Hōjō's plans. The smaller daimyō of the Kantō had now been squeezed into extinction, or had submitted as vassals of the Hōjō. Ujiyasu now had to face the threat from other

24

successful families whose own territories bordered the Kantō, and who had built their own multi-provincial domains in much the same way as the Hōjō. The history of the next two decades became one of a series of fights, alliances and treaties between the three power-blocs of Hōjō Ujiyasu, Takeda Shingen and Uesugi Kenshin.

The latter two names were every bit as formidable as the Hōjō, but fortunately spent a great deal of time fighting each other at five successive 'Battles of Kawanakajima', so that their incursions against the Hōjō took the form of minor raids. We will refer to the Takeda and Uesugi many times in the pages to come. Both were innovative in their strategy and tactics, and the fact that they were so evenly balanced made most of their contests indecisive, leading a later generation of historians to dub their Kawanakajima encounters 'mock battles'. In fact they were no more mock battles than any of the encounters of the Sengoku Period, and the fourth Battle of Kawanakajima in 1561 (described by the present author in '*Battles of the Samurai*') had one of the highest percentage casualties of any battle in which samurai engaged.

Consequently, grand strategy became the most important martial art. It was strategy that took into account all the military necessities of knowing when to attack, where and with what, as well as less glamorous considerations, such as the making and breaking of alliances and treaties. There was still territory to be won by the giving of battle, but the prize changed from the winning of one castle, or even half a province, to securing control of two or three provinces at one stroke. The skilled strategist thus took a long-term view of warfare, conducting operations by outstretching the enemy

25

army and then cutting his lines of supply and communication. Thus the mark of a good daimyō was that he could field an army of well-trained samurai, who had received a reasonable amount of military training, without denuding his fields of agricultural workers. So prolonged, and so intense, were these 'little wars' that every available man was needed. It is at this stage of Japanese history that *ashigaru* (foot-soldiers) began to emerge as an important factor, but still only as a separate unit under well-disciplined samurai, as illustrated by the Takeda army in the *Kōyō Gunkan*:

Ashigaru taishō shū *(units):*
Yokota Juro'e 30 horsemen, 100 ashigaru
Hara Yozaemon 10 horsemen 50 ashigaru

Different areas of Japan called for their own tactical skills. The Takeda, for instance, carried out most of their offensive campaigns on the flatlands of Echigo and the Kantō, and accordingly developed a powerful cavalry arm, able to strike swiftly and heavily. They used cavalry as mounted spearmen, and the days of the élite mounted archer were seen no more. The spears could be carried as lances, or used for cutting from the saddle, the horseman leaning forward in his stirrups. A long-bladed *naginata* (glaive) could also be very effective in a charge.

The daimyō's castle
The symbol of the daimyō's power was the castle. It acted as a centre of the economic life of his territory, and provided defence in times of war. In this photograph, we are looking from within the castle walls to the battlements of Kanazawa castle.

26

The armour of the samurai also changed. No longer was it carried to the battlefield in a box and donned for combat; with long-drawn-out battles ranging over a wide area, the samurai had now to live and sleep in their armour. Thus, for example, whereas earlier armour had numerous silk cords holding it together, in the new conditions of warfare these collected lice, sweat and dirt, and complicated designs were abandoned. Samurai were still encouraged to emulate their ancestors, but the successful general in these warlike times thought not in terms of samurai but of samurai armies, and no individual glory, no noble deed, was to come in the way of the serious business of winning battles. Needless to say, old traditions died hard, and there are numerous instances of glory-seeking samurai all but ruining a carefully planned campaign in their pursuit of honour. The invasion of Korea in 1592 developed into a race between two rivals to see whose army could enter the capital first, and the preliminary campaign to the great Battle of Sekigahara in 1600 nearly collapsed when two generals each insisted on leading the assault on a vital castle.

The nemesis of Nobunaga

The bow, the original samurai prestige weapon, was relegated to specially trained *ashigaru*, who were most useful as sharpshooters. As for the majority of lower-rank soldiers, they acted as foot spearmen, or formed the numerous corps armed with the most devastating addition to the samurai arsenal – firearms. Firearms were introduced to Japan by the Portuguese in 1542, and were eagerly adopted. While supplies were still limited, they were prized as samurai weaponry; but as the nimbler swordsmiths converted their trade to that of a gunsmith, vast quantities were produced, and squadrons of *ashigaru* trained in their use. It was the ideal *ashigaru* weapon, as the minimum of training was needed to enable it to be fired with all the accuracy of which it was capable.

There were, no doubt, some daimyō to whom this comparatively crude weapon came to be looked on as inappropriate for a samurai. The gun, after all, equalised the lowest and the highest by demanding no greater strength, control or daring than it took to pull the firing mechanism or load a bullet. To a noble samurai it represented the encroachment of barbarian culture into that most traditional of all Japanese social arenas: the battle-field. It defiled both the possesser and the victim, who was thereby deprived of an honourable death. But daimyō who believed in these views tended to be either very rare, or dead. In practice, wars had to be won, and no major daimyō would dare to be without large numbers of firearms.

All that divided the daimyō on the question of firearms was the way in which they were used, and Hōjō Ujiyasu did not live to see the ultimate proof of their worth. He died in 1571, and four years later some sound military thinking, rather than social considerations, led Oda Nobunaga to his famous decision to line up three ranks of matchlockmen at Nagashino. The Takeda and the Hōjō had kept the *ashigaru* to the rear, or in small units under individual commanders, where their guns were less effective. Nobunaga's volley firing, on a large enough scale, tended to ensure that someone would at least hit something. The result was the destruction of the Takeda cavalry on a colossal scale, and a revolution in daimyō thinking.

It also established Oda Nobunaga as the first of the 'super-daimyō', who had begun to acquire some of the former Shōgun's notional powers. But for the Hōjō, the visible result of the lessons of Nagashino was an investment in the defensive architecture of their castles and the natural walls of the surrounding mountains. The destruction of the Takeda, which took until 1582, and the unexpected death of Uesugi Kenshin in 1578, which was followed by a succession dispute, both served to give the Hōjō tranquil borders. Following the family tradition, Ujimasa retired in 1577, leaving his son Ujinao with a false sense of security. From within their kingdom

Hōjō Ujimasa (1538–1590)
Ujimasa was the eldest son of Hōjō Ujiyasu and took part in all his father's campaigns. The turmoil in the rival families of Uesugi and Takeda gave Ujimasa a false sense of security, which was to be totally eclipsed in 1590 when Odawara fell to Hideyoshi's army.

of the Kantō they heard of Nobunaga's murder in 1582, and the take-over by one of his former *ashigaru*, Toyotomi Hideyoshi. Then they began to hear of Hideyoshi's conquest of western Honshū, his taking of Shikoku island, the astounding conquest of the vast southern island of Kyūshū, and by the time they had grown used to the idea that Japan had a new Shōgun in everything but name, an army of 200,000 men was encamped around Odawara castle.

The new daimyō

Here, in 1590, the story of the Hōjō as daimyō came to an end. The siege was long, but largely bloodless, and ended with Hideyoshi ordering the suicide of Ujimasa and the exile of Ujinao. The Hōjō territories were given to Hideyoshi's ally, Tokugawa Ieyasu, but within ten years their vanquisher was to die, leaving an infant to inherit, and with the Battle of Sekigahara in 1600 the great game of *go* was won, and Japan was covered with the playing-pieces of one daimyō – the Tokugawa.

All the existing daimyō had already submitted to Hideyoshi. Now they were forced to submit to the Tokugawa, and to their relief were allowed to keep their heads on their shoulders. In his wisdom, Tokugawa Ieyasu recognised the skills and systems by which these warlords had built up and governed their territories. Their petty kingdoms had been managed well, as we shall see in the chapters that follow, and Ieyasu saw the possibility of using the existing structures as part of his new domain, which was the whole of Japan. So the former warlords became the 'local government' of the dynasty he founded. The Japanese expression is the *baku-han* system,

A daimyō's procession
One of the subtler ways by which the Tokugawa Shōguns sought to control the daimyō was by the *sankin-kōtai*, or 'Alternate Attendance' system. This required the daimyō to leave their families in Edo, the Shōgun's capital, and alternate their own residence between Edo and their own *han* each year. The roads of Japan, therefore, witnessed a succession of gorgeous parades. These daimyō followers are from a scroll depicting such a procession, in the Hōsei-Nikō Kenshōkan, at Nagoya, and are reproduced here by kind permission of the curator.

which combined within it the best of centralised government through the Shōgun's *bakufu*, and the local duties of the daimyō's territory, or *han*. The price the daimyō had to pay was to be severed from their traditional provinces and to be settled elsewhere in Japan, where they had no local loyalties that could spark a rebellion. The first few years of the seventeenth century thus saw a colossal act of moving house. The *fudai-daimyō*, the traditional supporters of the Tokugawa, were given the provinces that controlled the most vital lines of communication. The *tozama-daimyō*, the 'outer lords' who had submitted after Sekigahara, or whose loyalty was felt to be less than total, were given domains far from their roots and far from one another.

The *baku-han* was a successful system that lasted until the Meiji Restoration and the establishment of modern Japan in the mid-nineteenth century. The Tokugawa family supplied a dynasty of fifteen Shōguns over two and a half centuries, supported by the descendants of the original daimyō warlords. We shall see in the pages that follow how they coped with the various demands made on them by peace and war to maintain the continued benevolent rule, under the Shōgun, of the daimyō, the 'Samurai Warlords'.

Focus of Loyalty

Throughout samurai history, whether in peace or in war, the daimyō had one outstanding role to play – to be the leader, to act as focus for loyalty, as through him the family, the clan and the domain were personified. A writer of the Edo Period put it succinctly: 'The relation of parent and child is limited to this life on earth; that between husband and wife continues into the after-life; that between lord and retainer continues into the life after that again.'

This vital loyalty took various expressions, many of which we will examine in the chapters that follow: self-sacrifice in battle, thorough and unspectacular management of a *han's* finances, following-in-death by the bizarre and wasteful act of suicide known as *junshi*, revenge for a beloved dead master, or total loyalty to a family in spite of a dishonourable heir whose conduct betrays the good name of his ancestors. But many of these expressions belonged solely to times of peace. In the Sengoku Period, loyalty required a mixture of the unspectacular and the dramatic, none more so than the total commitment to a defeated daimyō to restore the family fortunes. There is no better illustration of this than the 'Samurai of the Crescent Moon' – Yamanaka Shika-no-suke Yukimori.

The Samurai of the Crescent Moon

The name of Yamanaka Shika-no-suke Yukimori is one almost totally unknown outside Japan, and as the personification of samurai loyalty to a daimyō he deserves to be better known. Yamanaka Shika-no-suke risked his life for the restoration of the Amako family of Izumo Province, to whom the Yamanaka were related. He fought his first battle at the age of 13, when he took an enemy head, and met a tragic death at the age of 34, but by far the most famous episode occurred at the time of the destruction of the Amako family, when he is said to have prayed to the new moon (the 'three-day' crescent moon as the Japanese call it). He had been born on the fifteenth day of the eighth lunar month of 1545, the day of the most brilliant harvest moon, and believed himself to be a heavenly child of the moon. 'Burden me with the seven troubles and eight pains,' he prayed, a Buddhist prayer inviting the gods to place the suffering of the Amako family upon his shoulders.

The Amako had claimed hegemony over the Chūgoku, the south-western extremity of the main Japanese island of Honshū, at the time of Tsunehisa (1458–1541), but their sway declined over subsequent generations, until they were opposed by the up-and-coming Mōri Motonari (1497–1571) during the rule as daimyō of Amako Yoshihisa. There were many battles with the Mōri in which Yamanaka took part, and at the Battle of Shiraga Yamanaka Shika-no-suke led 200 mounted samurai, and carried out daring tactics of withdrawing calmly then returning to the fray up to

A samurai in formal dress
A daimyō's loyal retainer served him in times of peace as well as war. Here we see a samurai in his formal attire of *kami-shimo*, which consisted of a winged jacket (the *kataginu*) with matching *hakama* (trousers) over a *kimono*, as depicted by an actor at the Toei-Uzumasa Film Studios in Kyōto.

Yamanaka Shika-no-suke
This print by Kuniyoshi depicts
Yamanaka Shika-no-suke praying
before the crescent moon when he
made his vow to restore the fortunes
of the Amako family: a vow that
ended with his own death. For this
reason, Shika-no-suke is one of the
paragons of samurai fidelity, though,
sadly, he is little known outside
Japan.

seven times, against a large army that was running them hard. His military
fame was utterly without question, but was not enough to prevent the
Amako's castle of Toda-Gassan being captured by Mōri Motonari. The defeated daimyō Yoshihisa retired from the life of a samurai to become a
monk, and lived until about 1610, but his loyal retainer was not giving up
so easily. He gave his famous prayer to the crescent moon, and from this
moment on, in exile, Shika-no-suke's fight began to complete the restoration of the honourable family.

Detail from the Ōsaka Screen
In this detail from a painted screen, in the Hōsei-Nikō Kenshōkan in Nagoya, depicting the siege of Ōsaka castle in 1615, we see a mounted samurai advancing into the attack. He is wearing a white *horō* on his back.

As Yamanaka was only a clan vassal, it was vital for him to work through existing members of the Amako family. The most senior member of the family was a certain Katsuhisa (Yoshihisa's father's first cousin), who had long since been a monk at the Tōfukuji in Kyōto. Yamanaka contacted him and persuaded him to return to lay-life and bring together the remnants of the Amako. With Yamanaka as his military commander, they could now plan the restoration of the Amako territory. Yamanaka sensibly realised that it would be a mistake to attempt the recapture of Toda-Gassan castle. Instead he conducted guerrilla operations against the Mōri in various places. On one raid he was captured by Kikkawa Motoharu, but managed to trick his way out of the trap. In 1578 he went to Kyōto to seek alliance with the most powerful daimyō in Japan, Oda Nobunaga, and appealed to him for the restoration of the Amako.

At that time the Mōri and the Oda clans were in a head-on collision. The Mōri had been supporting the fanatical monks of the Ikkō-ikki against Nobunaga, ferrying in guns to their fortress at Ōsaka. To take on the Mōri on their home ground was a difficult proposition for Nobunaga, as they controlled most of the shipping in the Inland Sea, which could cut off any army advancing overland. To have an ally in the Mōri heartland was an attractive proposition, and Oda Nobunaga's general, Toyotomi Hideyoshi, was already in the process of capturing Kōzuki castle in Harima province. Once it was secured, Nobunaga allotted it to Amako Katsuhisa and Yamanaka Shika-no-suke, who were immediately besieged by the Mōri with a great army of 30,000 men.

At the time Hideyoshi had a Mōri general confined in his castle of Miki, and, hearing of the danger to the Amako, detached half his army to relieve them. But he was overridden, and received an order from Nobunaga to abandon Kōzuki castle to its fate. There were, apparently, more important strategic considerations than the fate of the Amako. Hideyoshi brought back the troops as they were. The Amako army was isolated and surrendered without the least resistance to the Mōri general, and Katsuhisa committed suicide. By this final act, the Amako were destroyed and obliterated. The loyal Shika-no-suke was taken prisoner and murdered in cold blood while under escort on the road at Takahashi in Bitchū province.

What are we to make of the story of Yamanaka? It is a strange tale of a daimyō's retainer having faith in the fortunes of a doomed family even when the daimyō himself had renounced the struggle. That Yamanaka eventually failed makes his efforts even more tragic, and so much more like the classic heroic failure, whose pattern we find throughout samurai history. There is a marked contrast here between Yamanaka and, say, the retainers of Takeda Katsuyori, hundreds of whom pledged service to Tokugawa Ieyasu when he was defeated in 1582. Yamanaka Shika-no-suke, with his stubborn adherence to samurai honour and the demands of loyalty, has a special place in the history of Japan.

The practical obligations of loyalty

Samurai history is dotted with similar examples of loyalty to a daimyō to the point of death, where a warlord's wishes were carried out in spite of extreme personal suffering. The above account shows this side of the nature of loyalty – the behaviour of the loyal retainer acting essentially as an individual; but the daimyō could not command a kingdom of individuals. There was more to being a samurai than fighting fiercely and loyally in battle. There had to be organisation, delegation of command, and discipline on the battlefield. In times of peace there had to be efficient administration, and a means for converting peace-time samurai into soldiers. The umbrella under which this happened was the *kashindan*, or retainer band, which was mentioned in the context of Hōjō Sōun. The samurai who served a daimyō in a *kashindan* were vassals in a highly developed feudal system. They held lands granted to them by the daimyō, in return for which they would fight his wars. As war was mercifully not a continual process, their services were 'retained', hence the word 'retainer' (in Japanese *kashin* or *kerai*).

Although the definition of a retainer could be made with precision, during the sixteenth century there was a considerable ambiguity and diversity about what constituted samurai status. The popular use of the term today, which usually embraces all Japanese warriors, was truer in the sixteenth century than it was at any other time in Japanese history, before or after. The overriding factor was the enormous increase in the numbers of men who called themselves samurai because they bore arms. Even though there was a great social difference between, say, the son of a daimyō, who had a horse, splendid armour and servants, and a minor part-time samurai from a village, each was part of the same system, which had as its primary function the aim of delineating the military obligation of each and every retainer. So, when war came, each retainer not only supplied devoted individual service, as in the example of Yamanaka above, but also supplied other men and equipment in proportion to the amount of income he received from his landholdings. There were two ways of expressing this in-

Rice fields and mountains
The basis of any daimyō's wealth was the yield of his rice fields, and this view, taken from the summit of Shizu-ga-dake in Shiga prefecture, shows how every bit of available flat land can be pressed into service.

Cooking rice for the army
We are reminded of the mundanities of command by this fascinating illustration from the *Ehon Taikō-ki*. A huge cauldron bubbles away, cooking rice for Hideyoshi's army, while sweating foot-soldiers poke the fire and unload straw bales.

come. The first was in terms of *koku*, which was the rice yield of the fields (one *koku* was 180.4 litres of dry measure, the amount that would theoretically feed one man for one year). Alternatively, as in the case of the Hōjō retainers, in *kanmon*, which was the cash equivalent. The resulting obligation was called the retainer's *yakudaka*.

The daimyō compiled registers of *yakudaka*. In the Hōjō's 1559 register (see Appendix I), the *Odawara-shū shoryō yakuchō*, the units (*shū*), which would make up the army in wartime, are delineated either geographically (for example, Izu-*shū* and Edo-*shū*) or according to a very broad functional definition (for example, *go-umawari-shū*, 'bodyguard', and *ashigaru-shū*, 'foot-soldiers'). There were also separate categories for the Hōjō relatives (*gokamon*) and allies (*takoku-shu*). There are several very good examples of the ratios of obligation used for *yakudaka*, which are missing from the Hōjō example. Asakawa's study of the Iriki family of Kyūshū quotes the muster of troops by the Shimazu daimyō when they attacked Takabaru castle in 1576. A 30 *koku* samurai had to supply personal service, plus one other; a 60 *koku* man added another follower, and so on up to 300 *koku*, who served personally, attended by ten other samurai. When Hideyoshi invaded Korea in 1592, the daimyō nearest to the embarkation port in Kyūshū had to supply six men per 100 *koku*, with lesser proportions from more distant supporters. The Jesuit François Caron, writing at the end of the Sengoku Period, noted that:

each of them must, proportionably, entertain a select company of Souldiers, always in readiness for the Emperor; so that he who hath a thousand koku *yearly, must bring into the field, when ever he is in command, twenty Souldiers & two Horse-Men.*

Thus the Lord of Hirado, who hath 60,000 koku *a year, must entertain, as he easily may, one thousand two hundred Foot, and one hundred and twenty Horse, besides Servants, Slaves, and what more is necessary for the Train.*

(The 'Lord of Hirado' at the time was the daimyō Matsuura Shigenobu 1549–1614.)

Such mobilisation orders could only work if the daimyō had the ability to survey his retainers' lands accurately and assess their value of income. As the sixteenth century progressed, the means for doing this became more sophisticated, and a daimyō acquired a very detailed knowledge of the location and extent of his retainers' holdings. It also gave the daimyō two additional powerful tools in ruling his domain. First, the *kandaka* meant that the retainer's relationship to the daimyō could be expressed in terms of income, rather than the mere possession of land. Great income meant great responsibilities, and the appointment to prestigious positions, such as *jōshu*, keepers of castles, and *bugyō*, magistrates.

Second, it made it much easier for a daimyō to transfer retainers from

Samurai resting in the castle
This unusual illustration from the *Hōjō Godai-ki* shows samurai polishing swords, playing *go*, and *sugoroku* (backgammon). One man is inspecting an arrow, while in the background sit their suits of armour and various weapons.

Hamamatsu castle
Hamamatsu castle covered a strategic section of the Tōkaidō road, and was owned by a succession of daimyō through the Edo Period as the Tokugawa Shōguns moved them from one fief to another. It had its most celebrated taste of action in 1572, when Takeda Shingen advanced on Hamamatsu and fought the Tokugawa at the Battle of Mikata-ga-Hara.

one set of lands to another. In particular it meant that a retainer's holdings could be split up geographically while still ensuring the same income. This reduced the risks of rebellion by retainers, as the lands, and therefore the people who worked them, were not a contiguous whole. It is also worth noting that retainers who were granted castles were given ones far away from their traditional territories. This, of course, was more pronouncedly so in the case of conquered enemies who had grudgingly pledged service.

To some extent, this anticipated the physical separation of the samurai from the land which was to be the hallmark of the Tokugawa class system. The retainers of all classes now identified themselves more and more with the daimyō, and less and less with the land they farmed. A relationship of dependancy developed as the retainer came to rely on daimyō authority to help him collect taxes from his lands. The relationship between a retainer and a daimyō thus gradually changed from one of independence and local identification to one of dependence and association with a great name. This was fine as long as the daimyō kept winning, but as the Takeda were to show dramatically in 1582, when a daimyō sneezed, the retainers caught a cold.

The élite retainers

Within every *kashindan* were an élite, a select group of senior retainers, called usually *karō* (elders). There are many surviving records of retainer

39

bands in the sixteenth century, most of which are arranged in similar ways under these élite persons. Our source for the Takeda is the list of retainers in the *Kōyō Gunkan*, which is itself based upon two earlier registers of Takeda retainers, one of 1567, which contains 235 names, and the other of 1582, which lists 895 surviving members of the Takeda *kashindan* who pledged service to Tokugawa Ieyasu following the destruction of Takeda Katsuyori by the combined armies of Oda and Tokugawa.

The Takeda *kashindan* consisted largely of three parts:

1   In the first place we have the *jikishindan*, or direct retainer band, who were divided into the *go-shinrui-shū* (relatives), the *go-fudai karō-shū*, the 'elders', and the leaders of the separate *ashigaru-shū*, the *ashigaru-taishō*.
2   The second main grouping was the *sempo-shū*, the unit for the surviving retainers of the many daimyō conquered by the Takeda, such as the Sanada family of Shinano.
3   The final section was the *kuni-shū*, the regional *bushi-dan* from the Takeda lands, who ranged down to village samurai.

Takeda Shingen was the leader of this 'Ever-victorious, invincible, Kōshu Warband', as he called it, of which the élite core were the hand-picked leaders, magnificent in action, of whom 24 brave and fierce individuals became well known as the 'Twenty-Four Generals'. The *Kōyō Gunkan* records Shingen's criteria for a good general, which laid as much stress on peace-time work as on the field of battle: 'Concerning honouring the exploits of great generals, first, (they must be) persons of judgement, second, (they carry out) punishments in the province, third, they achieve great victories in battle, we honour their fame in these three.'

The 'Twenty-Four Generals' is, in fact, not a contemporary term, but one invented later. The Japanese as a race seem peculiarly fond of numerical categories, and the 'Takeda Twenty-Four Generals' is a popular concept from stories and illustrations. The selection of the 24 relates to their popu-

The Takeda 'Twenty-Four Generals'
Every daimyō had an élite corps of senior retainers. In the case of the Takeda family, the élite were the so-called 'Twenty-Four Generals'. The term is not contemporary, and different illustrations depict different individuals. This scroll is in the Memorial Hall on the site of Nagashino castle.

larity with the masses in the Edo Period, and we see them in the portraits included in three painted scrolls of the Twenty-Four Generals, on which there are various faces of generals. The commander-in-chief Shingen is painted in the top centre, and 24 individuals are arranged to left and right in two rows. The 24 generals join Shingen and Katsuyori, and Shingen's younger brothers Nobukado and Nobushige are shown in various ways.

I have examined these scrolls carefully, and discovered that there are, in fact, 33 individuals represented. Furthermore, some of the greatest names in the Takeda hierarchy are not included at all. One example is Hajikano Dene'mon Masatsugu, an *ashigaru-taishō*, or general of *ashigaru*, a demanding post, who added his own unique chapter to the Takeda legend, when in 1569 Takeda Shingen led his army against the Hōjō. On approaching Odawara, the Takeda army was met by a swollen river. Shingen ordered his army to stop while the depth was tested, and Hajikano volunteered for this dangerous task. He drove his horse into the angry waters and began to swim it across. So deep was the river that at one time all that could be seen of Hajikano was the *sashimono* banner on his back, which bore a design of a playing piece from the Japanese board game of *shōgi*. Hajikano's piece was the spear, which in *shōgi* can only move forwards, a reason he put forward to Shingen for his confidence in advancing!

Another strange omission is Morozumi Bungo-no-kami Masakiyo. Masakiyo is said to have been the youngest son of Takeda Nobumasa, and was therefore Shingen's great-uncle. He is believed to have been 81 years old at the time of his death at the fourth Battle of Kawanakajima, and held the rank of *ashigaru-taishō*. Shingen had, in fact, made this old general *honjin-hatamoto*, 'headquarters-samurai', for the battle, a comparatively safe position, but the headquarters was attacked in a surprise charge by Uesugi Kenshin. The old general drew his sword, plunged into the enemy and was killed. Shingen bitterly regretted his death, and Morozumi is one of only three Takeda generals to be buried at Kawanakajima.

Other names surprise one by their inclusion. Anayama Baisetsu and Oyamada Nobushige are included but, after years of service to Shingen, these two later betrayed his son Takeda Katsuyori. Nevertheless, the concept of the 'Twenty-Four Generals' remains a popular one, and they can

---

A daimyō in command

The great warlord Uesugi Kenshin sits with his generals to receive a message from a wounded scout. As Kenshin was a Buddhist monk he wears the traditional white headcowl. Behind him fly the three banners that always indicated his presence: the red rising sun on blue which was the treasure of the Uesugi house; the elaborate version of the character for 'dragon', which was always raised on the battlefield as his army went into an attack; and on the viewer's right the character *bi*, the first syllable in the name of Bishamon-ten, under whose divine protection Kenshin lived, which was flown at his headquarters on a battlefield.

His generals, accompanied by retainers carrying their personal banners, sit beside him. From left to right, they are as follows: Shimojō Saneyori (white ring on red), who was in the forward division at the fourth Battle of Kawanakajima in 1561; Takanashi Masayori (chequerboard); Nakajō Fujikashi, who received a personal commendation from Kenshin for his action at Kawanakajima, has the red flag with white designs; Honjō Shigenaga has the bold character *jō*; and Suda Chikamitsu, also of the forward division, has the gold swastika.

The wounded samurai bears the Uesugi *mon* of love-birds on his *sashimono*, which identifies him as a retainer of a member of Uesugi Kenshin's family, or of someone regarded as equivalent to a family member.

be found represented at the festivals held every year in the area around Kōfu, Shingen's old capital. Many others of the famous daimyō of the age had their 'number of generals'. Tokugawa Ieyasu had 16, Uesugi Kenshin either 14, 17 or 28, depending on which version you read.

One factor that was common to the generals on both sides, as indeed it was to many powerful daimyō retainers of the period, was the giving of honorific titles. In addition to their surname and given name, they tended to be known as 'Feudal Lord of...'. The surprising thing about these titles, which appear in Japanese as '...*no kami*' is that they frequently refer to territories not actually owned by the clan in question, and often hundreds of miles away. Shingen's great-uncle, Morozumi Masakiyo, was '*Bungo no kami*', the nominal feudal lord of Bungo province on the island of Kyūshū, over a thousand miles to the west, and which probably none of the Takeda had ever visited. Other titles reflect nearby territories controlled by other daimyō which the retainer's overlord coveted. Baba Nobuharu, one of the most skilled to the 'Twenty-Four Generals', was *Mino no kami*, Mino province being a possible future gain for the Takeda as part of an advance on Kyōto. At one time, there were living no less than three prominent samurai all bearing the identical title of '*Suruga no kami*'. One was Katō Nobukuni, a general of the Takeda who had responsibility for the teaching of archery; another was an Uesugi general, Usa Sadayuki, the truce-bearer

The 'Twenty-Four Generals' at Shimobe
Every May, the Takeda 'Twenty-Four Generals' are brought to life in the *Shingen-kō* Festival at Shimobe, in Yamanashi prefecture. The character on the far end of the line is Yamamoto Kansuke, easily recognisable by his buffalo-horn helmet. The 'generals'' names are painted on their *sashimono* banners, which would not have been done in the sixteenth century.

after Kawanakajima, and the third was a retainer of the Mōri daimyō in the west of Japan – Kikkawa Motoharu. None had any direct connection with Suruga province, which was actually owned by the Hōjō.

In spite of all the honorific titles, feudal obligation and rewards, not all lord-vassal arrangements succeeded, even among the élite. There were, in fact, some spectacular failures, such as Sasa Narimasa (1539–88). He was one of Hideyoshi's most senior retainers, granted a fief of 100,000 *koku* in Etchu province, but when Hideyoshi was opposed by Oda Nobuo in 1584, Narimasa backed Nobuo, and was chastised by his former comrade, Maeda Toshiie. Hideyoshi dealt with Narimasa with the great generosity that was his hallmark, and transferred him to a new fief in far-off Higo province in Kyūshū in 1587, giving Narimasa then following warning as he did so:

1   *To the 53 local magnates the same fief as before is to be granted.*
2   *No land survey shall be made for three years.*
3   *Due precaution is to be taken never to embarrass farmers.*
4   *Due precaution is always to be taken that no insurrection shall take place.*
5   *No charge shall be made upon farmers for the contribution to the public works to be carried out at Ōsaka.*

The above are strictly and carefully to be observed.

Unfortunately Sasa Narimasa betrayed the trust Hideyoshi put in him, and was 'invited' to commit suicide.

The lord's horse
Two samurai attendants wait with the lord's horse outside the *maku*, the curtained enclosure used to screen the field headquarters of a daimyō. The *mon* on the *maku* is the chrysanthemum-on-the-water design of Kusunoki Masashige. This is a further section from the scroll of Kusunoki's career owned by the Nampian Kannon-ji at Kawachi-Nagano, and is reproduced here by kind permission of the Chief Priest.

The call to arms

With a call to arms, the *kashindan*, with its detailed records of obligation, was transformed from a paper army into a fighting force. An example relating to the year 1557 has been preserved in the archives of the Uesugi family. It is in the form of a highly detailed letter, which is not surprising considering that the man who is being summoned is Irobe Katsunaga, Kenshin's *gun-bugyō*, a rank equivalent to Chief of Staff. He lists the disturbances attributed to Takeda Harunobu (Takeda Shingen) and warns Katsunaga of the dangers to the province of Shingen's belligerence:

Concerning the disturbances among the various families of Shinano and the Takeda of Kai in the year before last, it is the honourable opinion of Imagawa Yoshimoto of Sumpu that things must have calmed down. However, since this time, Takeda Harunobu's example of government has been corrupt and bad. However, through the will of the gods and from the kind offices of Yoshimoto, I, Kagetora have very patiently avoided any interference. Now, Harunobu has recently set out for war and it is a fact that he has torn to pieces the retainers of the Ochiai family of Shinano and Katsurayama castle has fallen. Accordingly, he has moved into the so-called Shimazu and Ogura territories for the time being....My army will be turned in this direction and I, Kagetora will set out for war and meet them half way. In spite of snowstorms or any sort of difficulty we will set out for war by day or night. I have waited fervently. If our family's allies in Shinano can be destroyed then even the defences of Echigo will not be safe. Now that things have come to such a pass, assemble your pre-eminent army and be diligent in loyalty, there is honourable work to be done at this time.

With respects
Kenshin,
1557, 2nd month, 16th day

A celebratory banquet
In this page from the *Ehon Taikō-ki*, a group of senior retainers feast after a victory. Their food is served to them on lacquered trays, and the *saké* is flowing freely!

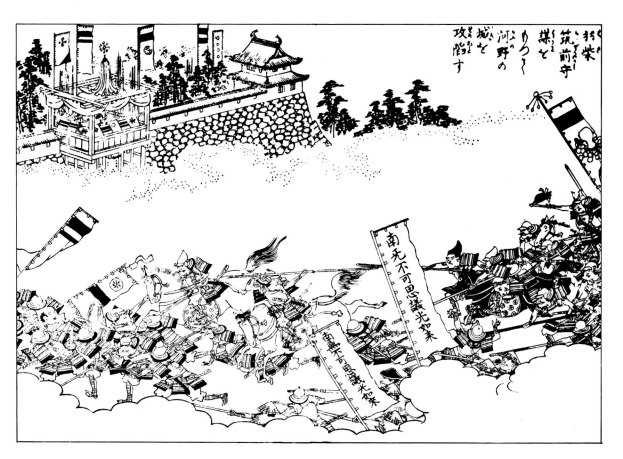

柴犬
筑前守
楽と
やりつく
河野の
城を
攻陥す

Hideyoshi attacks a castle
Here the *Ehon Taikō-ki* shows
Hideyoshi's troops neutralising an
opportunistic attack by the defenders
of a castle, identified by the caption
as Kawano.

Needless to say, less important retainers received a less imposing call to arms and, in the case of the part-time samurai of the countryside, a general proclamation would suffice. The well-known example from about 1560 of the call to arms against Uesugi Kenshin by Hōjō Ujimasa (though sealed by his retired father Ujiyasu as the young daimyō was off campaigning) has sometimes been ridiculed as evidence of his lack of concern for the quality of his troops. In contrast, it shows the universality of the definition of samurai referred to above, and his willingness to reward any who serve him well:

1 All men, including those of the samurai class in this country district, are ordered to come and be registered on the 20th day of this month. They are to bring with them a gun, spear, or any kind of weapon, if they happen to possess one, without fearing to get into trouble.
2 If it is known afterwards that even one man in this district concealed himself and did not respond to the call, such man, no matter whether he is a bugyō *or a peasant, is to be beheaded.*
3 All men from 15 to 70 years of age are ordered to come; not even a monkey tamer will be let off.
4 Men to be permitted to remain in the village are those whose ages are above 70 years, or under 15 years, and too young to be used as messengers, but the others are all ordered to come.
5 It will be good for the men to prepare for the call by polishing their spears

and preparing small paper flags to be taken with them. Those who are fitted to be messengers, and desire to do that service, will be so permitted.

6   All the men covered by this order are to come to Katsukui on the 4th day and register before the lord's deputy and then return home...if the appointed day happens to be rainy they are to come the first day the weather is settled. Men must arrive at the appointed place properly armed with anything they happen to possess, and those who do not possess a bow, a spear or any sort of regular weapon are to bring even hoes or sickles.

7   This regulation is generally applicable, and even Buddhist priests who desire to do their duty for their native province are ordered to come.

It is ordered to pay strict attention to the implications of the above seven articles, and if there be anyone who disregards this ordinance and neglects his duty, such a one is to be severely punished; while the man who is careful and eager to be loyal to his lord will be rewarded with the grant that is reasonable and suitable to him.

By such means, the sixteenth-century warlord assembled his army. The obligation of loyalty was fulfilled in part. It could now be tested on the battlefield.

Commander-in-Chief

When the samurai clan went to war, the daimyō's role became that of transforming this retainer band with its patterns of loyalty into an efficient fighting unit on the battlefield. The daimyō thereupon assumed the demanding role of commander-in-chief of the domainal army.

Setting off to war

Setting out for war
This picture from the *Ehon Taikō-ki* shows the meticulous preparations made when an army set out for war. Armour is removed from boxes, bamboo flagpoles are threaded through the banners and, in the left foreground, an attendant fixes a samurai's *sashimono* into place on the back of his armour.

Once the troops had been assembled, the actual process of setting out for war was attended by much ceremony, whether it was for a long campaign, or as a farewell ritual immediately prior to the start of a battle. There are copious records of the form these rituals took, which have provided the basis for the re-enactments of such ceremonies in the former castle towns of noted daimyō. I am well acquainted with two of these – the Uesugi *Butei shiki* at Yonezawa, which re-enacts the departure ceremony of Uesugi Kenshin, and the *Shingen-kō matsuri* at Kōfu, which is part of a number of

commemorative events for Takeda Shingen. (I have also had the unique privilege of being invited to play the part of Shingen's general, Baba Nobuharu, at the latter celebration in 1986.)

In ancient times, according to Japanese legend, a battle would customarily begin with a blood-offering to the gods of war in the form of a human sacrifice, either a captured prisoner or a condemned criminal, though there does not appear to be any written evidence for such practices continuing beyond the eighth century AD, and certainly during the time of the samurai the blood-sacrifice is confined to the offering of severed heads after the battle, rather than an actual sacrifice beforehand. Nevertheless, the need for prayers to the gods of war, of whom the most important was Hachiman-dai-Bosatsu, the deified spirit of the Emperor Ōjin (201–312) and tutelary deity of the Minamoto clan, permeates much of the ritual surrounding departure for war and victory ceremonies.

The ceremony of departure was centred around the practical need for a review of troops. With his army drawn up ready to march off, the daimyō would sit, surrounded by his generals in a semicircle, against the backdrop of the *maku*, the large curtains used to screen the headquarters position from view. In the case of Uesugi Kenshin, who was a Buddhist monk, this would have been preceded by his praying for victory within the shrine of the Buddhist deity Bishamon-ten inside Kasuga-yama castle. Only then would Kenshin go out into the courtyard to take his seat with his generals.

Four Generals at the Nagashino Festival
A general's military costume was often embellished by the wearing of a surcoat, called a *jinbaori*. The four men here are taking part in the annual Nagashino Festival.

There he would partake of the traditional farewell meal, served to him with great dignity. There were three dishes, *kachi-guri* (dried chestnuts – probably included for no reason other than the literal translation of the characters used is 'victory chestnuts'), *kombu* (kelp – a basic ingredient in Japanese cooking) and prepared *awabi* (abalone), all three of which were regarded as bringing good fortune. He would also drink *saké* (rice wine), served within three cups, one inside the other. The number three was also regarded as bringing good luck from the divinations of yin and yang geomancy, and the three cups represented heaven, earth and man.

When the army was ready to move off, an attendant would tie the commander's sword round his waist, then his quiver of arrows (rarely encountered in the Sengoku Period) after which the daimyō would stand up, take his signalling fan and receive the shouts of his assembled troops. There were various ways of doing this, but there are two shouts in common – the first being 'Ei!' (Glory!), to which there is given the response 'Ō!' (Yes!). In the *Shingen-kō-matsuri*, the man playing the part of Shingen's *gun-bugyō*, Yamamoto Kansuke, orders the other generals to raise their swords, and calls, 'Ei! Ei! Ō!', to which the generals reply, 'Ei! Ei! Ō!'. In the Uesugi version, it is 'Kenshin' himself who calls 'Ei! Ei!', and his generals reply, 'Ō! Ō!' repeated twice. This shout was also given at the end of a successful battle. (There is a splendid example in Kurosawa's film *Ran*.)

Traditionally, the general would then mount his horse, put on his helmet, and the flags would be raised. Just before the procession moved off, a Shinto priest would bless the army with the chanting of *sutras*. Uesugi Kenshin would also re-dedicate to Hachiman the 'Hachiman-bow' which was a treasure of the Uesugi. After this, Kenshin would mount his horse, surrounded by his three banners: the Bishamon-ten, a red rising sun on blue (a gift from an emperor), and the 'warring dragon' flag, which led a charge by the Uesugi samurai.

Organisation on a battlefield

Armies were controlled on the battlefield using a range of visible and audible signalling methods. Of the latter, the most important were the *taiko*, the big war-drums and the *horagai*, the conch-shell trumpet. War-drums varied in size from the very large specimens mounted in the open-work towers of castles, to ones carried in a frame on a man's back. In the eighth chapter of the *Hōjō Go-dai ki*, we read: 'The *horagai* was blown when a battle plan was put into disorder. Similarly on hearing the voice of the *taiko* the soldiers would regroup...'

In another section of the *Hōjō Go-dai ki*, we hear of the use Hōjō Sōun made of a *yamabushi* who was adept at playing the *horagai*:

The soldiers obeyed the commands of the horagai, *and those proclaimed by the* taiko. *There was a* yamabushi *called Gakuzenbo of Ōyama in Sagami [province]. He took the Buddhist name of Satsuma, and possessed a large* horagai. *This* yamabushi *was especially skilled in blowing the* horagai. *It could be heard for a distance of 50* chō *[about six miles!]. When Hōjō Sōun set out to war this* yamabushi *came from the Ōyama temple. He was [made] a* hatamoto *and blew the* horagai. *It is said that his descendants blow the* horagai *to this day.*

Horagai were also used for time-keeping.

The use of flags to identify and control units of troops was based on a very sophisticated use of heraldry. Prior to the sixteenth century, heraldry in Japan had not gone much further than the straightforward identification of an army. Now it became the means for subdividing and controlling an army, made necessary by the need to control large bodies of troops. My study of the army of the Shimazu shows how the troops fielded by the Shimazu grew from 3,000 in 1411 through 5,000 in 1484, to an estimate of possibly 115,000 at the siege of Minamata in 1576. Even during the straightened circumstances forced upon them by Hideyoshi's defeat of them in 1578, they were still able to supply 10,600 warriors for the Winter Campaign of Ōsaka in 1614. Complex manoeuvring of such numbers, such as the early morning clash during the fourth Battle of Kawanakajima (1561) between the Takeda (16,000) and the Uesugi (13,000) also presupposes quite sophisticated methods of troop recognition and signalling, in addition to well-rehearsed drill and discipline. Also, armour was becoming uniform in style, and the gradual introduction of armour protection for the face, which within the century was to develop into a complete mask, made the need for quick identification more pressing than ever. The response to this was a considerable development of the use and design of flags, notably in three forms: the *nobori*, the *uma-jirushi*, and the *sashimono*.

The *nobori* is the familiar form of long vertical flag, supported along the

Blowing the horagai
The *horagai*, the conch-shell trumpet, was an important signalling device in armies of the Sengoku Period. Here a *horagai* is blown during the Nagashino Festival by a man dressed as an *ashigaru*.

52

top edge, which can be seen everywhere in Japan today, from shops to temples. Its military use seems to be well established by the third quarter of the sixteenth century, and several contemporary painted screens show a great profusion of *nobori*, many of which have *mon* (family badges).

The *uma-jirushi*, literally 'horse insignia', was introduced to distinguish the person of a general, which was the function of the European 'standard'. According to regulations introduced early in the Edo Period, a daimyō with an income of 1,300 *koku* or over was entitled to a *ko-* (small) *uma-jirushi*, held by one man, while those with 6,000 *koku* and over could have an *ō-uma-jirushi*, which required two or three people to hold it. A samurai 'standard-bearer' would either have the *uma-jirushi* seated in a leather pocket at the front of his belt, or strapped into a frame on his back. In the case of the *ō-uma jirushi* the other two men would hold on to separate tethering cords.

The *uma-jirushi* did not always take the form of a flag. Several three-dimensional objects were used, such as a large red umbrella by Oda Nobunaga, and the *sen nari hisago* or 'thousand gourd standard' of Toyotomi Hideyoshi. Of the flag versions, one well-known example is Uesugi Kenshin's red sun disc on dark blue. The flowing *hata-jirushi*, popular in earlier centuries, continued to be used in armies, and in the case of Katō Kiyomasa (1562–1611) served as his *uma-jirushi* in the form of a long white banner with the Nichiren motto *Namu myōhō renge kyō*, which is preserved in the Hommyō-ji in Kumamoto.

The sashimono

The real innovation in heraldic display in the sixteenth century was not in the use of large flags but in the introduction of a personal banner for the

The sashimono of Tadano Samon
See overleaf for the account of how this particular *sashimono* inspired a comrade in the heat of battle.

Detail from the Ōsaka Screen, showing sashimono
The *sashimono* was the most important addition to Japanese heraldry during the sixteenth century. It consisted of an identifying device, usually a flag, fixed to the back of a suit of armour. This picture is from the painted screen of the siege of Ōsaka in the Hōsei-Nikō Kenshōkan at Nagoya.

individual called the *sashimono*, and worn on the back, its shaft slotting into a specially constructed carrier. Two cords ran under the armpits from the *sashimono* shaft to two rings on the front of the armour, to help hold the flag in place. *Sashimono* sometimes bore the *mon* of the commander, though there were many exceptions, as we shall see, and some cases where the *sashimono* was not actually a flag at all but a three-dimensional object.

Two examples of the use of *sashimono* appear in the chronicle *Meiryō Kohan*: 'At the time of the Ōsaka campaign there was a retainer of Kii Raisen called Yabe Tora no suke, of great strength with a *sashimono* of length two *ken* [12 feet!], and a long sword over three *shaku* [3 feet].'

The second extract shows how a striking *sashimono* could inspire a comrade:

There was a retainer of Satake Yoshinobu called Tadano Samon. He was expert in the ways of horse and bow, spear and sword, and furthermore became a samurai of great bravery and strength.... At the time when this Samon went to the battlefield he wore a large sashimono. *The* sashimono *was a* nobori *of white cotton cloth on which was written in large characters, 'hitoashi-fu ko Tadano Samon' [Tadano Samon who will not take one step backwards]. There was once a time when the Sasaki army were defeated in battle. One of their common soldiers had lost heart and retreated, but when he was about to drink water from a stream by the road-side, he saw the great* sashimono *where it had fallen into the water. He saw the characters on it, and regretted that he had retreated. This mere footsoldier hurried back and charged into the midst of the great army of the enemy. He fought with*

Battle across a river
At the signal given by a bursting rocket, samurai ford a river into battle, under the covering fire of their arquebusiers. (From the *Ehon Taikō-ki*.)

 本
橡 元
寺 の
の 水
ひ を
あ
断つ

Smashing an aqueduct
A reliable water supply was vital to the defenders of a castle. In this illustration from the *Ehon Taikō-ki*, the besiegers of Chōko-ji castle are attempting to smash the aqueduct, having driven off the guards. It was the destruction of the aqueduct that led to Shibata Katsuie's final, desperate charge into the midst of the enemy. (See *Battles of the Samurai* by this author.)

great desperation and took three helmeted heads.... He ended his career with 200 koku.

The best evidence of the role heraldry could play on a battlefield is the Hōjō army under Hōjō Ujiyasu in about the year 1559. The *shū* units in the 1559 register, referred to in the previous chapter, are largely preserved on the field of battle, with great use being made of the heraldic *sashimono*.

Ujiyasu's army consisted of two major parts, the first being the troops supplied by his well-established and loyal family retainers, the 28 *roshō*. Of these the 20 *shōshō*, 'captains', formed the first rank, while behind them were the 8 *karō*, 'elders', five units of which were identified by the use of different coloured *sashimono*, and therefore called the *go-shiki sonae*, or 'five colour regiments'. Thus Hōjō Tsunanari (1515−87), the victor of the Night Battle of Kawagoe, led men with yellow flags on their backs; Hōjō Tsunataka wore red; Tominaga Masaie (who is recorded as the keeper of Edo castle in 1564) wore blue; Kasawara was white; and Tame, black.

It is almost certain that each of these coloured flags would bear in addition the Hōjō *mon* of the *mitsu uroku*, the fish-scale design, which is depicted on a red *sashimono* preserved in the Kanagawa Prefectural Art Museum in Yokohama. There is also a reference to black *sashimono* ('*sashimono* should be black and new') in a military ordinance issued by Hōjō Ujikuni (1541−97) in 1574.

The most fascinating use of heraldry in the Hōjō army is, however, found in the core of the army, the *go-hatamoto* 48 *banshō*. The 48 *banshō*, 'captains', were under Ujiyasu's direct command, and were divided into 6 companies of 7 *banshō*, and one of 6. Each *banshō* commanded 20 men, and every unit was distinguished by a single *kana* on his *sashimono*. The interesting point about this arrangement is that the seven units were grouped in accordance with the *i-ro-ha* syllabary. The *i-ro-ha* is a poem which contains every one of the phonetic *hiragana*, and is traditionally used as a way of teaching Japanese children their alphabet, so that the order was:

– *i, ro, ha, ni, ho, he, to*
– *chi, ri, nu, ru, o, wa, ka,*
– *yo, ta, re, so, tsu, ne, na*
– *ra, mu, u, i, no, o, ku,*
– *ya, ma, ke, fu, ko, e, te*
– *a, sa, ki, yu, me, n,*
– *mi, shi, e, hi, mo, se, su*

This meant that the *sashimono* of Ujiyasu's army spelled out a poem, which roughly translated, means 'Colours are fragrant, but they fade away. In this world of ours none lasts forever. Today cross the high mountain of life's illusion, and there will be no more shallow dreaming, no more drunkenness.' Among this group we know that a certain retainer called Nanjō Gemba-no-suke, along with his own men, wore the character 'u' on his *sashimono*.

There are few details regarding the heraldry of the other units, though one may assume that the allies (the *takoku-shū*) displayed their own *mon*. The *ashigaru-shū*, who were little regarded at this time, were kept in a homogeneous unit under reliable command, probably with little identification.

Heraldry and the Takeda

Hōjō Ujiyasu frequently found himself in arms against his belligerent neighbour Takeda Shingen, and there is considerable evidence of the use of heraldry by this renowned commander. The most important flag was a large *nobori*, preserved today in the Takeda Museum at the Erin-ji at Enzan (Yamanashi-ken), bearing in gold characters on blue the motto 'Swift as the wind, silent as the forest, fierce as a fire, steady as a mountain'. Other flags included what is now the oldest surviving 'rising sun' flag in Japan. He also had two long red *nobori* bearing Buddhist prayers, and a personal flag with three Takeda *mon* with 'flowery' edges.

Shingen also used heraldic devices to differentiate the various units of his army in a similar fashion to that of the Hōjō. Instead of the Hōjō use of colour and *kana*, the various units of the Takeda are distinguished by the flags of their commanders. There is little use of the Takeda *mon*, or indeed of any device resembling a *mon*. Instead there is a predominant use of bold design and colour. Two examples from the *go-shinrui-shu* are Takeda Nobutoyo, who used a black flag bearing a white sun's disc (Nobutoyo was the son of Shingen's younger brother Nobushige, who was killed during the fourth Battle of Kawanakajima in 1561, where it is believed he used the same flag), and Ichijō Nobutatsu, another of Shingen's brothers,

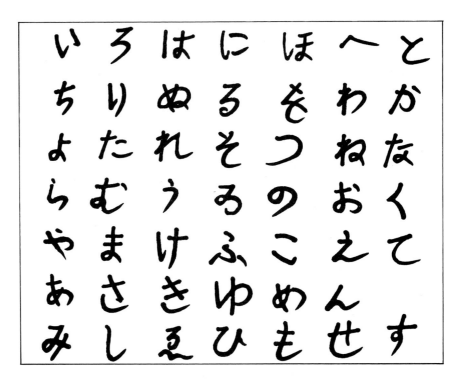

The flags of the Hōjō army, 1559
These are the *hiragana* characters used on the *sashimono* of the Hōjō army. (See text for full description.)

いろはにほへと
ちりぬるをわか
よたれそつねな
らむうゐのおく
やまけふこえて
あさきゆめみし
ゑひもせす

who had a flag divided horizontally into two halves, white on top and red underneath. From the *go-fudai karō-shū*, we find Baba Nobuharu, killed during the pursuit from Nagashino in 1575, whose flag was a black zigzag on white. All are displayed at the Takeda festivals (see pages 154–5).

Takeda Shingen's arch-rival, Uesugi Kenshin, is less fortunate in his present-day commemoration. Of his 'Twenty-Eight Generals' who are personified at the annual re-enactment, nine of the families died out during the Edo Period, and are therefore not recorded in the illustrated register of 1841, which the organisers of the *Butei-shiki* have used to reconstruct the

Kakizaki leads the charge of the Uesugi samurai

This plate illustrates the pivotal moment during the fourth Battle of Kawanakajima in 1561. The Takeda army had crossed the river in secret during the night, expecting the Uesugi army to come fleeing across their front after a dawn raid by a Takeda unit on their camp. In fact, the reverse happened. Guessing Takeda Shingen's plan, his rival Uesugi Kenshin had similarly transferred his army by night. As dawn broke, the Uesugi samurai pounced upon the Takeda flanks in a devastating charge.

The Uesugi vanguard was led by Kakizaki Kageie, whose *uma-jirushi* (personal standard) bore a large golden grasshopper, and whose samurai wore a *sashimono* charged with the unlikely sounding device of a giant radish! To their rear are the flags of Shimazu Norihisa (the same black cross as the better-known family of Shimazu in Kyushu), whose samurai accompanied Kakizaki in the charge, and in the distance appear the flags of two minor Uesugi retainers, Ōishi (star pattern) and Nozokito.

To the rear of the Takeda lines is the flag of Hara Toratane, whose position close to Shingen's headquarters meant that his soldiers received the brunt of the charge. The *ashigaru* in the foreground bear the Takeda *mon* on black, indicating that they follow a family member, namely Takeda Nobushige, Shingen's brother, who was killed during the battle. Note how the spearman carries his sword blade downwards, it being the only practical way for it to be carried if it is thrust through the belt and the wearer has to use a spear. (The author is indebted to Messrs. Bottomley and Hopson for this point of detail.)

flags used in the re-enactment of the departure for war of their favourite son. The 1841 register is extrapolated backwards to a register of 1575, which, unlike the Takeda list, gives no indication itself of flags, but has the additional advantage that it lists the weapon types to be supplied by each unit (see Appendix II). As they are heterogeneous collections, it is reasonable to assume that the Uesugi army, like the Takeda, fought in units under the banner of the commander. This is supported by the notes and illustrations which the festival committee kindly supplied to me. Once again, there is a minimal use of actual *mon*. Two of the most remarkable designs are recorded for Kakizaki Izumi-no-kami Kageie, leader of the Uesugi vanguard at the fourth Battle of Kawanakajima in 1561, who used a personal *uma-jirushi* of a golden grasshopper on a blue field, while his followers had red *sashimono* charged with a white *daikon*, the giant radish!

Heraldry and specialised units

In the three examples above, there seems to have been little use made of heraldry to indicate differing functions, other than the broad categories of *ashigaru, go-umawari-shū*, etc.; not that this is surprising, because the battle-field organisation of the time, being based on registers such as the Hōjō 1559 survey, relied on retainers supplying their own troops and fighting loyally for the daimyō. The one exception is the use of *sashimono* to distinguish the *tsukai-ban*, or messengers, whose role was a vital one in warfare. The Tokugawa *tsukai-ban* used a *sashimono* bearing the character *go* (the figure 5), and the Takeda *tsukai-ban* bore a centipede. The colours are variously described as being black on white, white on black, black on red, gold on black and gold on blue. The chronicle *Musha Monogatari* tells us a good story about the Takeda *tsukai-ban* which is interesting in that it illustrates the meticulous regulations in a daimyō's army, and also the refreshing discovery that samurai could have a sense of humour!

Takeda Shingen instructs one of his
tsukai-ban
The *tsukai-ban*, or messengers, were a vital arm of any daimyō's army. Here Takeda Shingen instructs one of his messengers, who has a centipede on his *sashimono*, at the second Battle of Kawanakajima, also known as the Battle of the Saigawa. (See *Battles of the Samurai* by this author.) This version is from a woodblock print in the author's collection.

Among the honourable [followers] of Takeda Shingen-kō, were the twelve o-tsukai ban. Their sashimono *were white flags with a black centipede. However, among them was a person called Hajikano Den'emon who wore a white flag without a centipede. Shingen-kō inspected them and questioned him why he did not have the same white flag* sashimono *as everybody else in the* tsukai-ban. *Shingen-kō got angry when someone disobeyed orders, and Den'emon had disobeyed military regulations. Den'emon showed a one* sun *[2.5 cm/1 in long] centipede that had attached itself to the loop of the* sashimono *under his armpit. Said Den'emon, if I attach it in place of the other centipede, I shall mingle with the other warriors, as it is like the others. Shingen-kō began to laugh.'*

This is the same Hajikano Den'emon Masatsugu whose use of a different *sashimono* design was described in the previous chapter.

The use of messengers and scouts was the most reliable way in which orders were transmitted and the units of an army controlled from the daimyō's headquarters. In the *Kōyō Gunkan*, we read that 'Sixty horsemen and one on foot from the samurai retainers of Itagaki were sent out as *o-mono miso* [scouts], but seeing no enemy approaching in the vicinity they returned. . . .' Membership of a *tsukai-ban* was highly regarded, as is indicated in the chronicle *Tosenkigyō*:

There was a retainer of the Echizen-Shōshō Tadanao called Hara Hayato Sadatane. He was originally a retainer of Takeda Shingen, but following the downfall of Takeda Katsuyori the Shōshō Tadanao, hearing at second hand of the fame of his

Warrior wearing a horō
The *horō* is surely the most impractical addition to a suit of armour ever devised. It consisted of a cloak on a bamboo frame, which took the place of the *sashimono* on the back of armour. It was often worn as an identifying device by messengers.

military exploits, engaged him [as a member of] the kuro-horō shu *[the 'black horō unit']. He served diligently as an army messenger.*

Note how the brave samurai is appointed to a responsible position, and that Tadanao's messengers were distinguished by wearing a black *horō*. The *horō* was a cloak-like bag, worn on the back of the armour, which was often stiffened with a basketwork cage, surely the most impractical item of military equipment ever devised, though even *sashimono* must have been a hindrance in the heat of battle. In fact, the painted screen in Hikone castle, depicting the Summer Campaign of Ōsaka, shows an *ashigaru* patiently holding a samurai's *sashimono* while the latter delivers the *coup de grâce*. Oda Nobunaga's retainer band included his own *go-umawari-shū*, which was divided into two parts: the red *aka horo-shū* and the *kuro horo-shū*.

The use of heraldry to distinguish such units presupposes a growing specialism of weaponry or tactics within a samurai army, and this was indeed slowly happening. The change from organisation based on feudal service to a more 'professional' army was a gradual development during the final quarter of the sixteenth century. Great impetus was given by Oda Nobunaga's victory of Nagashino in 1575, which owed a great deal to his use of *ashigaru* firing arquebuses against the advancing Takeda cavalry. This implies a considerable degree of discipline and shows how the use of *ashigaru* had developed. Their position at the very front of Nobunaga's army, rather than at the rear as in the case of Hōjō Ujiyasu's standard battle plan, is a striking difference. As his career progressed, Nobunaga became one of the first daimyō to issue his *ashigaru* with a simple, standard suit of armour, and there are many illustrations showing these *okegawa-dō*, and the lampshade-like *jingasa* helmets, emblazoned with *mon*, which became the typical *ashigaru* armour of the period.

One of the Takeda generals, Obu Toramasa, somewhat anticipated this future development in heraldry by dressing all his soldiers in uniformly coloured armour: a bright-red lacquer. Records tell us that this was common to all ranks, and included horse-harness and the *sashimono*, which bore a white crescent moon. Obu Toramasa's troops were known as the 'red regiment', thereby providing circumstantial evidence that the troops provided by such a retainer fought as one group under that general. They 'exploded on the enemy like a ball of fire', according to the *Kōyō Gunkan*. This was later adopted by his younger brother, Yamagata Masakage, and subsequently copied at the suggestion of Tokugawa Ieyasu by one of his chief retainers, Ii Naomasa (1561–1602). His 'red-devils', as they came to be known, are depicted on the painted screen of the Summer Campaign of Ōsaka, which is in the Ii Art Museum in Hikone. Incidentally, Yamagata Masakage was killed at Nagashino in 1575, and his troops wore a black *sashimono*.

Samurai with arquebus
The introduction, by the Portuguese, of firearms in 1542, was a major turning-point in the history of Japanese warfare. All daimyō used firearms, but few realised how effective they could be if employed in large quantities. This was demonstrated at the Battle of Nagashino in 1575, which is commemorated every year by the festival shown here, where reproduction arquebuses are fired from the site of the keep of Nagashino castle. The gunner is wearing full samurai armour.

The rituals of victory

Even more ceremony surrounded the celebration of victory than attended the setting out to war. After a battle, the victorious daimyō would reward his loyal followers. Great honour was attached to having taken the first head, though as mounted troops were able to return their trophies more quickly than foot-soldiers, the claims often had to be revised at a later

The Hōjō take Fukane
The taking of Fukane castle by the Hōjō army was attended by appalling savagery. The heads were cut off all the defending garrison, and displayed. This illustration from the *Hōjō Godai-ki* reminds us of the often savage and bitter nature of samurai warfare.

stage. There is, therefore, no shortage of written source material relating to brave exploits and head-taking in particular. One *kanjō* (letter of commendation) from Uesugi Kenshin and dated 1561, is addressed to Nakajō Echizen-no-kami Fujikashi, who died in 1568, praising his behaviour at the fourth Battle of Kawanakajima.

We departed on the tenth day of the ninth month, and at the time when we gave battle to Takeda Harunobu at Kawanakajima in Shinano, he was a person unparalleled in the earnestness of his efforts. It is a fact that relatives, retainers and even reserve troops, a large number of whom were killed in battle, were inspired to loyal military service. Even thought the rebels sent a thousand horsemen into the attack we won a great victory, an event that will give us satisfaction for many years to come. Futhermore, there was also much glory gained. These loyal exploits will certainly never be forgotten by the descendants of Uesugi Kagetora. We admire

*his military exploits all the more set beside the great importance of his loyalty,
which is not surpassed by anyone.*

A general account of the army's exploits was also valuable, as in the following fragment from the *Kōyō Gunkan*:

*Concerning the exploits of the samurai retainers of Takeda Shingen, in the first
place the spearmen met, [earning] fame for their lances, and renown when the
same ones grappled with and pulled down horsemen. We also praise the second
rank of spearmen.*

Most of the ritual surrounding a victory celebration concerned the bizarre
practice of head inspection, which we will discuss later, but for a retainer,

or an ally, alive and victorious, there were other more welcome privileges, as we read in the chronicle *Yamamoto Toyohisa-shiki*, which refers to the Ōsaka Campaign:

That night twenty-three heads were taken. At dawn on the seventeenth day twenty-four men were summoned before Hideyori . . . and received rewards of gold. One man called Kimura Kizaemon who had suffered a wound was given surgery.

Most daimyō appreciated the effects of hot-spring bathing for treating wounds, and general recuperation after a battle. The actual location of these hot springs was kept secret, as a wounded daimyō would be at his most vulnerable to an assassin. Takeda Shingen had three secret springs, one of which, at Shimobe in the mountains of Yamanashi prefecture, celebrates Shingen's use of its healing waters in an annual festival. The care Shingen took of his wounded is confirmed by the records of the Erin-ji. Four months before one of his five battles at Kawanakajima, he requested the monks to be ready to provide rest and recuperation facilities for the wounded.

The battle having been fought and won, the trophies taken and examined, the part-time samurai of the territory could now return to their fields, until by the end of the sixteenth century even this would stop, and even these lowly samurai would be warriors and nothing else, having no function in life other than to serve their warlord with loyalty and devotion in peace and war.

The wounded general at the healing spring
The beneficial effects of hot springs have long been known to the Japanese, and every daimyō had his own 'secret springs' where he could recuperate safely from wounds. Takeda Shingen had a secret spring at Shimobe, and his use of the healing waters is commemorated annually by a festival, where local people dress up as Shingen and his 'Twenty-Four Generals'. The man in the foreground represents Shingen himself, and wears a mock bandage.

The Cultured Warlord

It is sometimes difficult, when scanning the pages of the war chronicles of the sixteenth century, to appreciate that the samurai, and a daimyō in particular, was regarded as the supreme aesthete and the arbiter of good taste. How could the hand that wielded the bloody sword so readily caress the delicate surface of a tea bowl? This apparent dichotomy between the utterly barbarous and the utterly beautiful is one of the most difficult concepts to understand in the life of the samurai.

It is tempting to discern a certain national trait, an innate ability that comes simply with being Japanese, to translate the most functional of objects into works of art, even to weaponry and instruments of death. That most deadly of weapons, the Japanese sword, is well recognised as having an outstanding beauty of its own. Somehow the samurai appreciated that perfection of form and perfection of function went hand in hand, and that perfection of form required a commensurate elegance of behaviour that complemented the elegance of the surroundings. There is no doubt that the families of daimyō, if not all samurai, were trained as extensively

A musical interlude
Seated on an improbably dramatic crag, the great general Toyotomi Hideyoshi listens to music while contemplating the siege of a castle. As well as a drum and flute, he is entertained by two men playing the *shō*, an ancient Japanese form of 'Pan's Pipes'.

in matters of literature and aesthetics as they were in the arts of war. More than one daimyō likened the literary and the martial arts as being the two wheels of a carriage.

Patronage of the arts was one aspect of the daimyō life that we were not able to identify in the turbulent world of the Hōjō family, but the 'super-daimyō' of the latter part of the sixteenth century, of whom Oda Nobunaga and Toyotomi Hideyoshi are the outstanding examples, were also considerable patrons of the arts. They employed artists to paint the screens that divided room from room in their palaces, and commissioned potters to produce vessels for the tea ceremony. Their tastes reflected their wealth, enabling them to share in peaceful luxury when not fighting. It is to Hideyoshi that we owe the elevation of the tea ceremony to an art form. The tea ceremony consists of an aesthetic exercise performed around the simple pleasure of sharing tea with friends. It is at once ritualistic and artistic. It involves the aesthetic appreciation of the tea bowl from which the tea is drunk, the flower arrangement and the vase which complement it, and the overall design of the tea house and the garden. A rare tea bowl could be more welcome to a daimyō than a fine sword, and was frequently much more difficult to acquire.

Nobunaga was also a patron of the *Nō* theatre, and is recorded as having chanted some choruses from the *Nō* play *Atsumori* before setting off to the Battle of Okehazama. *Nō*, like tea and the contemplation of a cleverly designed garden, brought serenity in much the same way as did the practices of the meditative Zen sect of Buddhism, to which many samurai were attracted because of its inner tranquility. But the appreciation of taste gave

Tea house of the Gyokusen-En, Kanazawa
The performance of the tea ceremony was one of the highest expressions of taste enjoyed by the cultivated warlord. This is a side view of the exquisite tea house of the Gyokusen-En, a garden in Kanazawa.

the cultivated warrior more than a serene and a composed mind, however useful that may have proved on the battlefield or in conference. It was also the means that sorted the accomplished man from the common, that proclaimed a subtle ostentation that may sometimes have teetered on the edge of vulgarity, but never quite managed to slip off. This cultivation, this refinement, was the mark of true aristocracy, and was part and parcel of being a daimyō, of being an élite among the élite.

The fortress of beauty

All the wealth of Japanese art and architecture that has survived to our day – and there is a great deal of it – points to the fierce warrior as patron of the arts, exercising the remarkable skill, noted above, of being able to transform the functional into the beautiful. Take, for example, the development of the Japanese castle. There is no more beautiful example of military structure in the entire world, and yet these graceful buildings, which soar above sweeping stone walls, evolved largely through savage military necessity. A castle of the early sixteenth century, such as would have been known to an early daimyō like Hōjō Sōun, was either a *yamashiro*, 'mountain castle' or a *hirajiro*, 'castle on the plain'. In each case, the style of architecture, if such a term is applicable, was entirely subservient to the need for defence, and the construction of the means of defence depended entirely upon the fortress's location, and would follow the lines of strength. A *hirajiro* would make use of a river or a swamp. A *yamashiro* would make use of rocky crags, concealing trees, and the slope of the ground. I have visited the recently excavated site of Odani, the *yamashiro* of the Asai family, burnt by Nobunaga in 1573. The buildings of Odani were spread across two hills joined in a saddle, and there is good visibility from every level. Only on the top is there an expanse of level ground, where Asai Nagamasa had his great hall.

One influence of Nobunaga's victory at Nagashino in 1575 was the beginning of what was almost a defensive mentality among the daimyō,

The site of Odani castle
This overgrown patch of land on the top of the wooded hill of Odani was the site of the main hall of the *yamashiro* of the Asai family. A few stones are all that is left of the fortifications, which were burned down by Oda Nobunaga in 1573. Odani has recently been excavated.

69

leading to the establishment of the huge fortresses we see today. For the first time stone was used in their construction, the labour being assessed by and supplied to the daimyō in much the same way as he obtained military service from among his subjects. But the spate of castle building, which Japan witnessed from 1580 to about 1615, was only partly connected to the introduction and effective use of firearms. As domains grew, the careful balance between agricultural and military needs could be solved by a strict division of labour between military men and farmers, and it was the achievement of very powerful daimyō, such as Oda Nobunaga, to produce a corps of professional soldiers. The new castles, many of which survive to this day, were built as the economic centre of the territory. They were also built very large, so that, if necessary, the entire standing army of the daimyō could be sheltered within the vast encircling walls.

Nobunaga's own castle of Azuchi was the first, and the greatest, of this new trend. It was built to control Kyōto, but it was not built there, but on a rocky plateau overlooking Lake Biwa. Where Nobunaga's creation differed, even from its contemporaries, was in the lavish decoration that was applied to it, so that this great step forward in castle design intimidated as much by its appearance inside and out, as by its strong walls and its armaments. Sadly, Azuchi castle is no longer with us. When Nobunaga was murdered in 1582, Azuchi proved no more impregnable to excited looters and arsonists than any other castle that had suddenly lost its leader, and it was burned to the ground.

Several other castles have survived and, if one disregards those that have been rebuilt in ferroconcrete in the last 20 years, there is a wealth of material for study. Inuyama, which floats on a wooded hill above the

Inuyama castle
Inuyama castle, which seems to float over the Kisogawa, enjoys one of the loveliest settings of all Japanese castles. It is also one of the best preserved, and is unique in being the sole remaining Japanese castle still under private ownership.

Kisogawa, is a very fine example. It is the only castle in Japan still in private hands, and its owners, the Naruse family, have cared for it since it was given to their ancestor, the daimyō Naruse Masanari, whose father Naruse Masakazu (1538–1620) had fought for Ieyasu. The site received its first defences in 1440 as a *yamashiro*, for which it was ideally suited, and the present tower-keep dates from 1600, replacing an earlier one which suffered when Inuyama was taken during Ieyasu's Komaki campaign in 1584.

Although from the outside the keep appears to have three storeys, in reality there are four. The uppermost storey commands an extensive view from the balcony that surrounds it, but the first storey holds the most interest. The daimyō's 'audience chamber' is built into the centre of the room. It is of modest dimensions, and fitted with sliding doors at the rear, through which samurai could come to the lord's aid at speed. The wooden floor which entirely surrounds it is 3 m (10 ft) wide and called the *musha-bashiri*, the 'warriors' run'. The other floors share the same austere design of plain, dark wood; the floors being connected one to another via alarmingly steep staircases.

Interior of Inuyama castle
The daimyō's private quarters at Inuyama are surrounded by a highly polished wooden corridor, called the *musha-bashiri*, or 'warrior's run'. To the rear of the room are sliding doors, behind which armed guards could be concealed.

The castle town – a world in miniature

As the sixteenth century gave way to the seventeenth, the castle, standing alone, surrounded by bare ground, itself gave way to the castle town, the *jōkamachi*. The castle towns symbolised in their design the feudal hierarchy which the daimyō had created for themselves and their retainers. They

were ordered places which, by their physical layout, made a statement about the classes within society, and the nature of the cultivated daimyō.

Edo castle, the seat of the Shōgun, was surrounded by the residences occupied by the daimyō on their annual visits, the *yashiki,* which we shall study in more detail later. The daimyō's own castle towns back in the provinces were simply miniature versions of Edo. Around their castles, where the family, and some senior retainers lived, were the homes of the other retainers, their distance from the castle walls being in roughly indirect proportion to their rank. The higher retainers, the *karō,* were placed just outside the keep, within the castle walls proper; the lower were outside the walls, protected perhaps by a moat, or an earthen wall. Completely walled cities on the European model were unknown. Between the two groups of samurai retainers lay the quarters of the favoured merchants

A home of a retainer in Nagamachi, Kanazawa
The narrow streets of the Nagamachi quarter of Kanazawa disclose the tiny courtyard of a former samurai's dwelling. Stepping stones lead to the door from the more formal granite paving.

Garden of the Toyokawa Inari Shrine

This charming garden, within the extensive grounds of the Inari Shrine at Toyokawa, shows many of the classic features of the Japanese garden, a miniature landscape with which every warlord would be familiar. *Koi* swim in the pond, which has its edge set off with tightly clipped box bushes. An ornamental pagoda balances the background.

and artisans, most, if not all, of whom would be engaged in trading and producing the goods that were in demand from the samurai class. Outside the ring of lower samurai lay a quarter of temples and shrines, whose buildings acted as an outer defence cordon, and from where the roads could be sealed off and guarded. From the edge of the castle town began the fields of the farmers, who grew the rice to support those within the *jōkamachi's* boundaries.

The city of Kanazawa is one of the best examples of such a layout. Owing to its position far from the Pacific coast, Kanazawa was spared the bombing of the last war which destroyed the layout of nearly every other city of comparable size, and it is possible to walk round Kanazawa today, as I did in 1986, and appreciate at first hand the effort of town planning that went into its original design. Kanazawa was the territory of the Maeda family, whose founder was Hideyoshi's general, Maeda Toshiie (1538–99).

Their castle town is built on a high plain between the Sai and the Asano Rivers. At its centre are the remains of the old castle, whose outer walls now house the university. Only the huge Ishikawa gate and tower remind one of its martial past, but even these remains are considerable. Across the road from the gate is the Kenrokuen, which is now a public park but which until 1871 was the private garden of the Maeda daimyō. The Kenrokuen is one of the best examples in Japan of the formal landscaped garden, but its most eloquent tribute to the civil engineering skills of the day lie in the way in which its lakes and waterfalls are fed with water. Water is in fact channelled from a distance of 10 km (6 miles) away, where the Saigawa is tapped, a system that was built in 1632 and is still functioning perfectly.

The best surviving examples of the retainers' residences are found in the quarter called Nagamachi. Here are quiet courtyards and tiny gardens surrounded by mud and plaster walls roofed with tiles. Of the merchants' quarters, little remains except the names, such as Ishibikichō, 'stone-cutters' quarter' and Daikumachi, 'carpenters' quarter'. To reach the temple areas, you have to cross one of the rivers – a forceful reminder of how the religious buildings were deliberately situated as the outer lines of defence.

It is possible, having seen Kanazawa, to imagine how Edo must have looked to the early European visitors before fire, earthquake and war took their toll of the Shōgun's capital, the bustling city that became Tōkyō. How fascinating it must have been to have looked with the eyes of someone such as Thomas McClatchie, who recorded his impressions of the soon-to-be-destroyed daimyō mansions of Edo for the members of the Asiatic Society of Japan in December 1878:

In passing through the streets of the city of Yedo, and most especially in what is commonly termed the 'official quarter' lying inside the Castle moats, the attention of the visitor is particularly attracted by long continuous buildings lining the roadway on either side. These present towards the street an almost unbroken frontage, save where a few large gateways, composed of heavy timbers strengthened with iron clamps, interpose to relieve the monotony of the general style of architecture. The buildings mostly stand upon low stone foundations, surrounded by small ditches; the windows are barred, and the general aspect gloomy in the extreme. They often differ widely as regards size, shape, mode of ornamentation etc.; but there is yet manifest a general likeness, there are still noticeable many common attributes which at once serve to stamp them, to the observant eye, as structures of one and the same type. These are the nagaya, *or barracks, for retainers, which formed the outer defences of the* yashiki *or fortified mansions wherein dwelt the feudal nobles of Japan until the era of the recent Revolution in this country; and though now in many cases deserted, ruined and fallen into decay, time was when they played a conspicuous and honoured part in connection with the pomp and grandeur of the old feudal system which received its death blow only a half score years prior to the present date.*

McClatchie's article goes on to list how the amount of land available for the *yashiki* depended upon the income of the daimyō, as did the size and design of the building he might raise upon it. The rules are precise:

Kokushū daimyō – gate either detached, or else built into the nagaya; *two small side gates or posterns, one on either side, immediately adjoining it; two porters' lodges, situated just behind the posterns, built on stone foundations jutting out into the roadway for about three or four feet, and furnished with barred windows; roofs of lodges convex, formed of two slopes descending from a central roof ridge protruding at right angles from the wall of the* nagaya.

The outer wall of the Sanada mansion
The Sanada mansion gives us a good idea of the appearance of the daimyō's *yashiki* in Edo, none of which have survived. The outer wall is surrounded by a gutter, and windows project from the sides of the gateway.

There is nothing left in Tōkyō now, or even in Kanazawa, that gives us any indication of the appearance of these *yashiki*, which because of their associations are among the most important buildings of Edo Japan, but McClatchie's descriptions, and extant sketches of the buildings, are uncannily similar to a group of buildings in Matsushiro, a town in the mountainous Yamanashi prefecture. Matsushiro was the site of Takeda Shingen's Kaizu castle, of which the stone base alone remains, and was the fief

granted to the son of the Sanada, Nobuyuki, who served the Tokugawa. The complex of buildings which contain the Sanada mansion, its clan school and a fine garden, have survived almost perfectly, owing to their remoteness. Matsushiro is a sleepy little place a few kilometres from the city of Nagano, but has recently seen an influx of tourists, drawn there by a very successful television series called *Sanada Taiheiki*, which told the story of the division of the Sanada family referred to in a later chapter. The outer wall of the complex must be as near to the appearance of a *nagaya* as one can find, and in fact bears remarkable similarities to the actual *nagaya* depicted in a photograph of the Satsuma daimyō's *yashiki* in Edo, which was burned in 1868.

Further delights await visitors inside the grounds, as there is revealed to their eyes the perfect example of a daimyō's mansion, complete with landscaped garden. The nearby Sanada museum, with its rich collection of the daimyō's personal possessions, completes a unique time capsule of the Edo daimyō.

The journey of pride

The *yashiki* was a very private place, unsuited to ostentation or the flaunting of wealth, but nowhere was the pride and the good taste of a daimyō more on public display than when he travelled along the great highways of Japan to visit the Shōgun. The *yashiki* of Edo may have belonged to the daimyō, but he was only able to live in it one year out of two, the alternate year being spent back in his castle town. This *sankin kōtai*, the 'Alternate Attendance' system, was the most unusual, and the most successful, of all the means the Tokugawa *bakufu* were to devise for reducing the risk of rebellion from the warlords. In essence, the *sankin kōtai* was no more than kidnapping on a colossal scale, because the rule was that the daimyō's wife and children lived in the *yashiki* of Edo, while the daimyō himself alternated his residence between his fief and the capital. That was one aspect of it. The other was that the muster lists, which in times of war had regulated a daimyō's feudal oligations in terms of the supply of men and equipment for war, were continued into peace-time by prescribing the size and equipment of the retinue which the daimyō would be expected to have accompany him on his alternating trips. As stipends were fixed, and there were no fresh lands to conquer, the cost of the *sankin kōtai* kept the daimyō in a state of genteel poverty, and probably constant worry.

Certain daimyō with particular defence responsibilities were allowed a reduced commitment. The Sō daimyō on the island of Tsushima, which lies between Japan and Korea, only had to reside in Edo for four months in every two years. A similar concession applied to the little-known but strategically vital daimyō of the Matsumae family on the northernmost island of Hokkaido. In the early nineteenth century there were fears of expansion by Russia on to Japan's northern territories, and there was a tentative Russian incursion on to Matsumae's territory in 1807.

For other daimyō, the likelihood of any conflict was a remote possibility, but they still had to march at the head of a huge army, gorgeously dressed and ready for battle, either from their *han* to Edo or back again, once every 12 months. When the procession of the Maeda daimyō, the richest in Japan after the Tokugawa (their income was a staggering 1,250,000 *koku*),

The mansion of the Sanada daimyō
The azaleas bloom in the garden of the mansion of the Sanada family at Matsushiro, an outstanding expression of the aesthetic side of the daimyō's life. We are looking from the garden to the main set of rooms which comprise the mansion.

left Kanazawa in the years of the mid-seventeenth century, it consisted of no less than 4,000 samurai, but within a century the sheer financial burden forced a reduction in numbers to 1,500. There is a pathetic note in the account books of the Inaba daimyō referring to additional expenses encountered in 1852 after being overtaken by darkness in the Hakone Mountains. The daimyō suddenly found himself compelled to purchase 8,863 candles and 350 pine torches, as well as hiring extra porters and lantern bearers.

But if the *sankin kōtai* was a burden to the daimyō, it proved otherwise to his retainers. There was the prospect of a long, but not unpleasant journey, much of which, for most daimyō, would be along well-trodden highways. The two main roads linking Edo with Kyōto were Tōkaidō, which followed the Pacific coast, and the Nakasendō, which wended its way through the mountainous interior. As early as 1604, three decades before the *sankin kōtai* was introduced, a system of post-stations was introduced along the Tōkaidō, and by 1633 and efficient post-horse and courier system was completed, and reduced the travelling time for the 480-km (300-mile) journey from Nihombashi in Edo to Sanjobashi in Kyōto to a mere ten days. By frequent changes of horses, couriers could make the journey in three days. Needless to say, a daimyō's procession was conducted at a much more leisurely pace, making good use of the *Tōkaido Gojusan tsugi*, the 'Fifty-three stations of the Tokaido' made familiar from the prints of Hiroshige. (The Nakasendō had 69 post-stations.)

Each of the 53 post-stations acquired its own personality. Each had some famous site or historical association, such as an exceptionally long bridge, a hot spring or a dangerous river. Some towns were famous for their local

77

delicacies, others for their inns, their girls and their porters. The porters, the *kumosuke,* were available for hire to carry baggage or palanquins. Whatever the weather these 'tough guys' wore only a loincloth. They were notorious for their rude songs, their drinking and their gambling!

To a daimyō's retainer, the annual march was not a risky voyage into the unknown, but a familiar journey repeated year after year, and with details familiar even to those who had never set foot along its length. Numerous wood-block prints and popular literature painted a picture of the great road for any who cared to enjoy it at second hand. There is very little left of the original Tōkaidō today, as Hiroshige's road has disappeared under railway lines and motorways, but, here and there, there are small sections, now no more than footpaths, which the determined traveller can find. I walked along such a short stretch near Yumoto, on the way into the Hakone Mountains in Odawara, and within seconds modern Japan disappeared from sight and from hearing. The traveller on the mountainous Nakasendō is more fortunate, and can walk a full 8-km (5-mile) stretch of the old road which once echoed to the feet of samurai. The path lies between the villages of Tsumago and Magome, high in the wooded mountains above the Kisogawa. Both villages, now bypassed by a modern road, are exceptionally well preserved by consent of the inhabitants, and give you the most vivid glimpse of old Japan available anywhere in that country today.

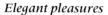

Street in Edo
A corner of the film set at the Toei Uzumasa Film Studios in Kyōto, showing a typical street of the Edo Period.

Elegant pleasures

One of the main attractions of the bustling city of Edo will be discussed in a later chapter, when we look at the notorious pleasure quarter of Yoshiwara. But there were other more seemly pleasures of which the daimyō and his family might partake during their sojourn in the capital. Where their appreciation of the arts differed from that enjoyed by their ancestors of the sixteenth century, who had invited artists and performers into their castles,

Garden of the post-station at Tsumago
This view is taken from within the main room of the post-station at Tsumago, looking out on to a simple, yet totally effective, Japanese garden. The ground cover is of moss, and the view is attractively framed by a split bamboo fence.

78

Masks for the Nō theatre

The *Nō* was the classical theatre of Japan, and the form of theatrical art that members of the samurai class were expected to patronise, unlike the vulgar *kabuki*. *Nō* actors wore masks, and a selection are shown here in this backstage photograph, which the author was kindly allowed to record.

was that the daimyō of the Edo Period could not claim much credit for patronage. The most notable cultural flourishing of the age occurred during the era-name of Genroku, which lasted from 1688 to 1703, and its impetus came largely from the newly wealthy merchant classes. The samurai class, and the daimyō in particular, may have pretended that the *chōnin* (townsfolk) were vulgar, of disreputable origin and with poor tastes, but by 1700 they had a century of tradition behind them, the wealth to enjoy artistic pleasures, and the confidence to commission them. So the culture which the daimyō enjoyed was one into which he was drawn, and which derived from a prosperous bourgeoisie devoted to amusement. The expression they used for it, *ukiyo,* the 'floating world', was a very telling one.

Hand in hand with the growth of *ukiyo* expression, 'samurai culture' went into something of a decline. There was little advance in architecture, probably because, as we noted above, the Shōgun's *bakufu* made rules for the size and shape of just about everything. Classical poetry all but disappeared, unable to compete for interest beside the vitality of the *ukiyo*.

The kabuki *theatre*

The year is 1713, and the renowned *kabuki* actor Ichikawa Danjurō II makes his dramatic entrance along the *hanamichi* as the hero Sukeroku during one of the first performances of the play *Sukeroku Yukari no Edo Zakura*. He wears a black *kimono* bearing the Sukeroku *mon*, while his *obi* bears in addition the actor's (Danjurō's) own family *mon*, a precedent followed by every actor in the role to this day. Sukeroku is an *otokodate*, a 'chivalrous fellow'. He is brave, charming and resourceful — all qualities that the townspeople looked for in a hero. In his

characterisation of the flamboyant Sukeroku, Danjurō even went so far as to wear a head-band and socks dyed with a certain indigo dye which, because of the huge cost of obtaining it from China, only the Shōgun himself was accustomed to using.

On the stage the ladies of the town await their hero's arrival. The villain Ikyū is not so pleased to see him! Two members of the audience squabble while their companions watch the actor's every move.

The *kabuki* theatre provided the townspeople of Edo with the ideal vehicle for examining the morals and behaviour of the samurai class. Several of the most popular plays were based on actual incidents in history, often ones that had occurred very recently. Family feuds, such as those within the Data and Maeda families, were included in the repertoire, although names and characters were always changed, and the plot elaborated almost beyond recognition. *Meiboku Sendai Hagi*, for example, which is based on the Date feud, includes a villain who can change himself into a giant rat! *Kabuki* was banned by the Shōgunate on several occasions, but its popularity ensured its survival.

The last bastion of true samurai aesthetics was the *Nō* theatre, which continued under daimyō patronage. The *chōnin* had their own theatrical art-form, the flamboyant *kabuki,* which attracted the samurai in droves. *Kabuki* was banned, totally ineffectively, on six occasions, and always bounced back owing to public demand and the willingness of the authorities to turn a blind eye. Its rewriting of recent history and current events, both elements of which were absent from the *Nō,* appealed to the samurai every bit as much as it did to the *chōnin.* Much use was made in the *kabuki* of general incidents which would have been familiar to the samurai, either from their actual experience, or from the traditions in which they were educated. For example, the play *Ōmi Genji Senjin Yakata,* first performed in 1769, contains a famous scene of a head inspection. *Mekura Nagaye Ume ga Kagatobi* re-enacts a real-life quarrel that occurred in Edo between fire-fighters employed by the Maeda daimyō and the official Edo fire brigade. The other great theatrical art of the age was the *bunraku* puppet theatre, where each large doll was manipulated by three men, producing the most amazingly lifelike effects. The *bunraku* was regarded as even safer than the *kabuki* for satire and the riskier sort of plot, and several *kabuki* plays began life as dramas written for the puppets.

The *Nō,* by contrast, took all its plots from ancient legend. The first Tokugawa Shōgun, Ieyasu, had been a great patron of the *Nō.* He had invited leading companies to Edo castle, and *Nō* performances were a regular part of important State functions. Some of his descendants took part in *Nō* themselves, which certainly kept them away from *kabuki,* and then in 1700 the arch-moralist of the day, Arai Hakuseki, in a severe attack of pomposity, pronounced even this most stately and restrained of theatrical forms to be deleterious to morality and a danger to the State. At a Shōgunal banquet in 1711, ancient music was substituted for the *Nō,* and from that time on the *Nō* lost much of its official prestige and the larger part of its samurai popularity. The tea ceremony went much the same way, degenerating into an empty ritual, far too complicated for the *chōnin,* and unable to compete with other delights awaiting the samurai.

Perhaps the fate of *Nō* holds the key to understanding the apparent paradox. During the Sengoku Period, there was a genuine need for the reassurance of nobility against the evidence of his own barbarism that the daimyō accumulated. Aesthetics gave reassurance. It soaked up the reality of their deeds in the same way as the spiked board and the cosmetics transformed a ghastly severed head into an object for neutral contemplation. Without the cultivation of art, and gardens, and theatre, the samurai would have gone mad. Then, when wars had ceased, the samurai class had nothing to prove to anyone. Their social position was firmly established and, apart from a few rare exceptions, they did not kill. Instead, they were stultified within a stagnant culture, from which the new merchant classes, with none of their inhibitions, were to liberate them.

However, as we noted earlier, to the first daimyō there was no paradox. The two aspects of the samurai life not only could coexist, they had to coexist. One could not be a successful daimyō without both, as Hōjō Sōun wrote in the last words of his 'Twenty-One Articles':

It is not necessary here to write about the arts of peace and war . . . for to pursue these is a matter of course. From of old, the rule has been, 'Practise the arts of peace on the left hand, and the arts of the war on the right'. Mastery of both is required.

An actor performing kagura

Kagura is a form of dance-drama which was the forerunner of the Nō. Performances are quite rare nowadays, but a particularly fine rendering is given annually by the villagers of Shimobe in Yamanashi prefecture, as part of their annual festival. The kagura is performed on a stage at the Kumano Shrine in the village. This photograph was taken at the 1986 performance.

Notwithstanding the fact that the Hōjō had little time for practising purely aesthetic pleasures for their own sake, and that their emphasis on the arts of peace concentrated almost totally on good government, there is no better summary of the duties in peace and war of the cultivated warlord of Japan.

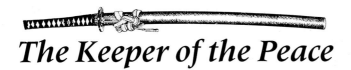

The Keeper of the Peace

During the Edo Period, one of the most important duties delegated to a daimyō, as part of the *baku-han* system, was the keeping of the peace and the administration of justice within the *han*. In this, the daimyō would find the reality of the streets of his castle town to be very different from the theoretical world of ordered and cultivated society which was the ideal. He would often find himself faced with a fire-trap of a city, where subservience to samurai was a myth, and where his own men would find

The daimyō presides
This page from the *Hōjō Godai-ki* neatly illustrates the daimyō's social position, as he receives gifts from his retainers. The daimyō sits on an elevated dais, while those lower squat on the *tatami*.

themselves in opposition to well-organised gangs of swordsmen every bit as well trained as well armed, and who owed equally firm allegiance to their own variety of Japanese warlord.

In theory, at any rate, this was a situation that could not possibly exist, because according to law, to established precedent and to a century of tradition, members of the samurai class were the only people allowed to carry swords. It was the wearing of swords that defined a samurai, as his privilege and his right. A series of edicts, beginning with Hideyoshi's famous 'Sword Hunt' of 1587, had set this trend in motion, and had theoretically disarmed all but the samurai class. In practice, swords, and other weapons, were readily obtainable and well used, sometimes by criminals, otherwise by desperate gangs of lower-class citizens upholding their rights and their lives against the abuse of power by samurai.

The samurai police

It was a very unusual daimyō, however, who failed to recognise the reality of life in Tokugawa Japan, and every daimyō was helped in his peace-keeping role by a well-developed police force. In common with many other institutions of Tokugawa Japan, the nature of the *baku-han* system allowed a successful system for the Shōgun's direct retainers in Edo to become the norm for the whole of Japan, and by 1631 the organisation of policing in Edo was replicated on a smaller scale in every *han* in the country.

As a daimyō spent much of his time travelling to and from Edo, he would delegate a major degree of responsibility within his own castle towns to magistrates, known as the *machi-bugyō*, who combined within their role

The seat of the Shōgun
In the Shōgō-In in Kyōto, this ornate audience chamber is preserved, with its characteristic raised dais.

the functions of chief of police, city mayor and presiding judge. In Edo there were two *machi-bugyō*, the need for two being similar to that which produced the system of two consuls in ancient Rome – each one kept an eye on the other! These two *machi-bugyō* worked a 'shift' system of one month on-duty, one month off-duty, though as the duties became more onerous in the expanding cities, particularly Edo, the 'off-duty month' became no more than a welcome quiet time for writing reports and seeing to other essential paperwork.

The Edo *machi-bugyō* had daily liaison with the Shōgun's senior councillors in Edo castle, which alone indicates the high status of the position. Even though the post of *machi-bugyō* was earmarked for comparatively lowly retainers of 500 *koku*, it carried an additional allowance of an extra 3,000 *koku*, and a court rank equivalent to that of some daimyō.

Under each of the two *machi-bugyō* were the *yoriki*, or assistant magistrates. There were 50 *yoriki* in all in Edo, 25 under each *machi-bugyo*. They were chosen from the Shōgun's direct retainers who had an income of 200 *koku*, and, in the case of the Edo *yoriki*, the appointment became hereditary within certain families, the position of *yoriki* passing from father to son. This resulted in a 'police force' that was very familiar with its territory, but also one that became very much a caste unto itself, living in a social limbo between the townspeople whose lives they controlled, and the samurai of the castle. The latter would have nothing to do with them because of the ancient Shintō fear of pollution from people who had a connection with death, as the *yoriki* had with the execution of criminals. In fact, the *yoriki* did not actually carry out executions; that was left to the outcast *hinin*, the 'non-humans', but the mere association with such practices, and their own fierce pride, kept the *yoriki* apart. The proud *yoriki* would wear a full samurai costume of the wide *hakama* trousers and the *haori* jacket, and wore the two swords of the samurai. They had a reputation for smartness in appearance, particularly in their hair-styles.

Serving under the *yoriki* were the *dōshin*, who played the role of the policeman 'on the beat'. They wore tight-fitting trousers rather than *hakama* and only carried one sword, though they were regarded as being of samurai status. In Edo, there were 120 *dōshin* under each *machi-bugyō*, and they were instantly recognisable by a distinctive side-arm that was a badge of office and a vital defensive weapon. This was the *jitte*, a steel rod fitted with a handle, and with one or two hooks along the edge of the 'blade'. Its purpose was to catch a sword stroke so that a felon could be taken alive.

The *dōshin*, accompanied by several assistants from among the townsfolk, who ranged from public-spirited citizens to paid informers, thus maintained the visible 'police-presence' on the streets of the castle towns, the *yoriki* being called to the scene of an arrest only if the situation warranted it. In this case, the *yoriki*, dressed in light body armour, would supervise affairs from horseback, with a spear kept as a last resort. The emphasis was always on taking the prisoner alive, which was no mean feat should the felon be an accomplished swordsman, as we shall see later in this chapter. Japanese ingenuity, however, allowed for the obvious danger and, in addition to the *jitte*, the *dōshin* were armed with a range of fierce-looking hooked and barbed spears, which kept the swordsman at bay, pinned him into a corner, or could usefully entangle items of clothing as he tried to escape. The determination of a cornered criminal was legendary, and many would sell their freedom as dearly as a samurai would sell his life.

The main street of Tsumago
The miraculously preserved main street of the village of Tsumago gives the best illustration of a village street from the Edo Period. It lies on the old Nakasendō road, which linked Kyōto and Edo (now Tōkyō) along the alternative mountain route.

Once the man was cornered and disarmed, he was rapidly tied up, and there existed a whole specialist area of 'martial arts' techniques for quickly and securely roping suspects. There is a famous wood-block print by Kuniyoshi depicting the arrest of a criminal by *dōshin*, which James Field has used for his picture on page 88, that brings the whole process of justice vividly to life. It is an illustration to a scene from a popular novel, first published in 1814. The hero, Inuzuka Shino Moritaka, takes to the roof of the Hōryūkaku temple to avoid arrest by the *dōshin*. There are several versions of the scene, where Moritaka seizes one unfortunate *dōshin* by putting his arm round his neck, as his companions thrust their *jitte* at him, and blow whistles, while their more nervous companions wait below with bamboo ladders, ropes and sleeve entanglers.

Making an arrest

This plate is based on a vivid woodblock print by Kuniyoshi depicting the arrest of a criminal by *dōshin*. It is an illustration to a popular novel entitled *Nansō Satomi Hakkenden* by Takizawa Bakin (1767–1848). The plot of the novel concerns with the exploits of eight brothers, one of whom, Inuzuka Shino Moritaka, ends up on the roof of the Hōryūkaku temple. He is pursued by *dōshin* armed with *jitte*, the peculiar 'sword-catchers', and other devices designed to facilitate arrest. They are dressed in typical fashion, with fitted trousers rather than *hakama*, thus freeing their legs for such exploits as climbing roofs.

The popular image of the wandering lone samurai owes much to the activities of the criminal element in Edo society. The same is also true of the martial arts, which are often regarded as the preserve of the ruling samurai class. In fact many martial arts techniques owe their development to farmers and townsmen, deprived of the right to carry weapons, who turned to the use of simple weapons and bare hands to defend themselves against any abuse of power by their betters. (See *The Lone Samurai* by the present author for a detailed consideration of these points.)

The resulting punishments which the *machi-bugyō* had in their power to dispense ranged in severity up to death – including crucifixion, for such crimes as murder. For a samurai, the death penalty could, on occasions, be carried out by the convicted man himself in the honourable act of suicide, called *seppuku*. In certain cases, the execution of a condemned criminal could be a means of testing the quality of a sword blade – making a more realistic alternative to the more usual *tameshigiri* performed on a corpse. There is the story told of one such condemned man who went to his end with remarkable coolness, telling the sword tester that if he had been forewarned that this was how he was to die he would have swallowed some large stones to damage the samurai's precious blade. A much lighter punishment was exile, which had been used for centuries in Japan as a way of dealing with offences of a political nature.

The great benefit of the *dōshin* system lay in its capacity for crime prevention. To the *dōshin's* local knowledge was added a topographical system that divided Edo into tightly controllable *machi*, or wards. This arose from the original design of the city, which was deliberately intended to make an approach to Edo castle difficult for an attacker. Like other big cities, the castle was surrounded by mazes of streets where the *chōnin* (townspeople) lived, and each *machi* was physically separated from others either by canals, walls or fences. It was thus a simple matter to control movement from one *machi* to another by means of gates which were fastened at night, and anyone passing through had to have appropriate authorisation.

Corporal punishment
A swift punishment for offenders from the lower social orders was a sound thrashing. Here, in an illustration to *Miyabu gaikotsu tobakashi*, the felon is held down securely while he receives his punishment under the watchful eye of the *yoriki*.

The brave otokodate

If areas of a city, such as Edo, could be sealed off from outside, they could also be well defended from within, and it is not surprising to hear of the development of organisations of townspeople to provide protection against

House in Tsumago
One of the many houses of Tsumago which convey the feeling of a past age. The wooden slats filter the bright sunlight from the dusty street.

rivals, or against samurai who neglected their code of conduct. Against the *hatamoto-yakko*, or samurai gangs, there developed the *machi-yakko*. They became very well organised in the Edo Period, and their leaders, styled *otokodate*, became famous. The word *otokodate*, 'chivalrous fellows', implies the resistance to authority by those of lower class. In fact, some of the great *otokodate* were originally of the samurai class and had become *rōnin* for various reasons, and moved to find employment in distant towns. One such was Banzuin Chōbe'e, 'Father' of the *otokodate* of Edo.

Banzuin Chōbe'e was originally from Higo province in Kyūshū, and was a retainer of the Terazawa clan of Shimabara, the scene of the great Christian upheaval of 1638, known as the Shimabara Rebellion. Following the suppression of the revolt, he felt Kyūshū as a *rōnin* and went to Edo, where his talents were soon put to use. He became a *warimoto*, an agent who acted as a go-between for acquiring labourers. Once established in Edo, Chōbe'e took the name of Banzuin, which was the area where he lived, and set himself up as a 'Godfather' of *warimoto* who acted particularly as agents for supplying carriers and other labourers to daimyō undertaking their annual pilgrimage to Edo to pay respects to the Shōgun. Chōbe'e received 10 per cent of the labourers' earnings as commission, and in return provided for them in times of sickness. Banzuin Chōbe'e, therefore, came to exert the same authority over his followers as a daimyō did over his samurai, which came in very useful when the townspeople were oppressed by the samurai *hatamoto-yakko*.

In the enforced idleness of the Edo Period, boredom and poverty turned many samurai into criminals. Groups with names such as the *Shiratsuka-*

Retainer's house in Nagamachi, Kanazawa
In contrast to the simple houses of Tsumago, this town house in Kanazawa reflects the type of architecture that would have been enjoyed by the retainers of the Maeda daimyō of Kanazawa. This house, in the Nagamachi quarter, is one of the best known in the city.

gumi and *Jingi-gumi* formed and caused violence. The city people 'hated them like scorpions', according to one Japanese historian, and their unreasonableness against the townspeople became proverbial. Because such violence and perverseness among the samurai could not be crushed by the townspeople alone, former *rōnin*, such as Chōbe'e, became the natural nucleus for opposition. As their confidence grew, the *otokodate* of the *machi-yakko* began to walk openly in the streets in defiance of rules forbidding them swords. At the same time, they developed the art of combat with other weapons, such as the the long, 2-m (6-ft) staff, or *bō*, and the shorter 1.5-m (4-ft) long *jō*. They also became accomplished in the art of the *tantō* (dagger), which could be concealed under clothes, and the defensive use of implements such as the *tessen*, the iron war-fan.

Greatness has its penalties. Chōbe'e's fame was considerable, which brought him into direct opposition to the boss of the powerful *hatamoto-yakko* called the *Jingi-gumi*, one Mizuno Jūrōzaemon. Jūrōzaemon was of senior samurai rank, worth 2,500 *koku*, and had the reputation for being something of a dandy (the Japanese term is *datemono*) dressing in the finest clothes.

One day, according to a popular tale, it was rumoured that Chōbe'e was in the vicinity of Yoshiwara, where Jūrōzaemon's party was meeting. Jūrōzaemon desired some iced *soba* noodles and, as Chōbe'e was in a *soba* shop, he proposed, after some ritualistic bragging, that Chōbe'e should buy him some *soba*, knowing already that the shop had sold out of *soba* and did not have a steamer. It was a neat way of humiliating Chōbe'e, but, nothing daunted, Chōbe'e went downstairs and gave one of his followers a considerable sum of money, and ordered him to buy up all the cold *soba* that was available, which the *machi-yakko* members proceeded to dump unceremoniously in front of Jūrōzaemon. As the huge pile grew, Jūrōzaemon realised that he could not get the better of Chōbe'e and retired with considerable loss of face.

Not long afterwards, one of Chōbe'e's followers, called Iida no Nibe'e, caught three of Jūrōzaemon's men making unreasonable demands of a drunken townsman. He set on them and threw them into a ditch. This increased Jūrōzaemon's bad feelings for Chōbe'e, and resolved him to invite Chōbe'e into a trap. The treacherous means whereby Mizuno Jūrōzaemon planned to dispose of Banzuin Chōbe'e, and the latter's willingness to walk into the trap for the sake of his honour, forms the basis of the greatest of all legends of the brave *otokodate*. It is quoted as an example of how the honour of a townsman could be every bit as noble as that of a samurai. In fact, Chōbe'e's determination to carry out the inevitable drama reminds one of the decision of Kusunoki Masashige to fight the Battle of Minatogawa because it was the wish of the Emperor, even though he knew the situation to be hopeless.

The evil Jūrōzaemon invited Chōbe'e to come to his house for a drinking party as a way of saying 'thank-you' for the gift of *soba*. Chōbe'e guessed that it was a trap, but went along nonetheless. He was attacked by two of Jūrōzaemon's men as he entered, whom he defeated, but before they began to drink together Jūrōzaemon invited Chōbe'e to take a bath, a common enough courtesy to a visitor. Once Chōbe'e was in the bath-house, Jūrōzaemon's men began to stoke the boiler to raise the temperature of the hot tub and scald him to death. As the hot steam rose, Chōbe'e tried to break out, but Jūrōzaemon had locked the door. With his

The murder of Banzuin Chōbe'e
Banzuin Chōbe'e is the great hero of the *otokodate* of Edo, both from his championing the cause of the townspeople against unruly samurai, and his violent death in a bath-house, where he was treacherously murdered by Mizuno Jurozaemon, his great rival from the samurai.

rival cornered within, Jūrōzaemon's men thrust spears at him through the partition. One spear pierced his leg and broke off at the shaft. Chōbe'e had no weapons on him and was surrounded by about ten spears. One then struck him a mortal blow under the ribs and the pitiful Chōbe'e, a spear through his chest, ended his days in a bath-house, in a manner every bit as noble as the samurai he had once been.

The unofficial daimyō

Crime was by no means confined to Edo, nor was the capital the only place where non-samurai ruled as petty daimyō over their criminal or lower-class kingdoms. The eight provinces of the Kantō plain, the large area of flat land that nowadays accommodates metropolitan Tōkyō, Yokohama and the Chiba peninsula, and extends northwards towards Nikkō and the Pacific coast, acted as a cradle for the criminal element towards the end of the eighteenth century, when crime was on the decline in Edo itself. Hoodlums were rampant in the Kantō provinces, because police power was dispersed in the complexity of Crown land, daimyō land and *hatamoto* land. The *yakuza* (gangsters) gathered there for making money. Kōzuke in particular was a centre of *yakuza* activity.

The nature of the locality of Kōzuke had made it a centre of textile manufacturing, and it was also well known throughout the whole country

A gambling den
The provision of gambling places was one of the main reasons for the growth of criminal gangs in the Edo Period. Here, in an illustration from *Tsūjin san kyoku-shi*, a group of men settle themselves for a session, refreshed by tea and tobacco.

for its hot springs. In earlier days, the recuperative qualities of hot springs were privileges known only to the upper reaches of the samurai class, as we noted earlier in connection with the treatment of wounded, but as the Edo Period wore on, the wealthier among the merchants, who already knew the value of hot baths, gained access to these pleasures. The taking of baths in 'spa-towns', where the mineral waters had healing properties, thus became a popular way of relaxing, as it is today for all Japanese, and hot-spring resorts vied with each other in the quality of their mineral waters and the range of comforts and entertainments they could provide. The spas of Kōzuke were convenient places where the textile wholesalers and healing-spring guests could resort for relaxation and amusement, and one pastime appealed above all others – gambling.

The provision of gambling dens promised immense profit for those willing to take a risk and, as they were operating in a very shadowy area of legality, it is not surprising that controlling gambling became an activity for

A fight in a gambling den
This lively sketch from *Miyabu gaikotsu tobaka-shi* depicts the violent end to a gambling session. Coins fly everywhere, and a dagger is drawn in anger.

organised crime. The gangs acquired territories in which their law held sway, much the same as the Sengoku warbands had developed into daimyō territories. The leaders of these gangs acquired the airs of daimyō themselves. Some of these gang leaders, especially those of samurai origin, acquired such a reputation for swordsmanship and command that they were employed by the civil authorities to teach swordsmanship to samurai.

At that time, the great swordsmen of the day, who were not hereditary samurai retainers of daimyō could be divided into two types: those who worked for the existing authority, hiring to them their swords and their skills, and those who by choice or by pressure of circumstances lived outside the law as outlaws. The outstanding example of the former was a man called Ōmaeda Eigorō. He comes over as something of a 'Godfather' figure, like Edo's Banzuin Chōbe'e, attracting to his side many of the young men who were to make their names in the criminal world of the Kantō provinces. Like the samurai, these bosses worked on a well-established hierarchical model of a 'father-figure' at the top, to whom followers held allegiance.

Ōmaeda Eigorō was a native of Kōzuke province, and killed his first man at the age of 16, a person called Kugo no Shōhachi. He went on to become a dependable and charismatic leader who influenced a generation of swordsmen, yet he was always careful to operate within the law. He was certainly not a murderer, unlike some of his disciples, and did not needlessly start quarrels. The *han* authorities found him very useful, and were ready to co-operate with him to gain some share of the enormous influence he exerted. His service to the civil authorities was as reliable as any samurai of the Sengoku Period, and he deserved his leader's stipend. His duties included teaching swordfighting, as he was a fencing master of the Nenryū *dōjō*.

The Battle of the Tonegawa Dry-River-bed
Iioka no Sukegorō and Sasagawa no Shigezō were two rival gang-bosses in Shimōsa. Their feud exploded into violence in 1844, in an encounter on the dry river-bed of the Tonegawa. Blades flashed in the moonlight in a battle as fierce as many of the skirmishes of the Sengoku Period. (From a woodblock print in the author's collection.)

A later example of another successful 'unofficial daimyō' is Shimizu no Jirochō, who acquired the title of the 'First Boss of the Tōkai'. Like Ōmaeda Eigorō, he built his territory on gambling, and developed his remarkable leadership skills through evading the numerous traps set for him by *yoriki* and rivals alike, until he achieved a quasi-official position within his own province. He died in 1893, his life having encompassed the final days of the Japanese warlords, most of whom he outlived.

The outlaws

On the opposite side of the coin from Ōmaeda Eigorō and Shimizu Jirochō, both of whom either co-operated with the authorities, or learned how to handle them, stood characters such as Kunisada Chūji (1809–50). Chūji never sold out to the samurai, and his exploits in resisting authority, retold in numerous plays and novels, made him something of a 'Robin Hood' of Japan. He was certainly a popular subject for fiction, and the romantic gloss of works such as '*Yagi bushi*' disguising the unattractive reality of a long catalogue of extortion and murder for which he was finally arrested and crucified in 1850 at the age of 41.

Kunisada Chūji's criminal acts may have caused great problems to the civil authorities of the day, but at least his expressions of rivalry were on an individual level. Two other 'pupils' of Ōmaeda Eigorō collided on a much larger scale, one of which produced a virtual battle that brought back echoes of the samurai wars of the Sengoku Period. It happened in another

of the Kanto provinces where crime flourished – Shimōsa. Shimōsa bordered the Pacific Ocean, and the fishing industry predominated, exerting a similar economic influence as the textiles of Kōzuke. The fishing industry of Shimōsa was centred around the port town of Chōshi, at the mouth of the Tonegawa with its huge flat river-bed. Around Chōshi, two leaders had their spheres of influence. Their names were Iioka no Sukegorō and Sasagawa no Shigezō. Neither was a samurai, and their surnames merely refer to their localities, as the possessive adjective 'no' indicates. Sukegorō was based in the present-day town of Iioka, and Shingezō held authority in Tōshō by the Sasagawa.

Iioka was a prosperous fishing port on the coast. Tōshō was also a bustling river port, 19 km (12 miles) away on the Tonegawa. Sukegorō is referred to in a Japanese account of his life as a 'sumo delinquent' (!), and a vagrant, at one time employed by Iioka no Amimoto as a fisherman. In course of time, he pledged loyalty to a gang leader, called Chōshi no Gorozō, from whom he received an enormous stipend, and whose territory he inherited.

In contrast to Sukegorō, Shigezō was born and raised in a large farming family of the area. His sphere of influence was handed over from a leader called Shibajuku no Bunkichi of Hitachi. Sukegorō was, in general, the senior of the two rivals, and Shingezō also looked up to Sukegorō but gradually, as their spheres of influence grew, respect gave way to wariness. Their territories grew rapidly during the early 1840s, and eventually the two spheres of influence reached their limits. Both men were of equal standing. Sasagawa no Shingezō acted first, and like his contemporary Kunisada Chūji, hatched a plot to murder Iioka no Sukegorō. However, Sukegorō got to hear of the plot and acted first, attempting to destroy his

rival on a grand and dramatic scale by carrying out a night raid on the Sasagawa headquarters on the south bank of the Tonegawa in the ninth month of 1844. The sight of this frenzied mass swordfight by moonlight has inspired some fine wood-block prints, and one particular work of literature, *Tempō Suikoden.*

By all accounts the raid was a ferocious affair, with all the hallmarks of a medieval battle. It even had its fallen hero, in this case a certain Hirate Miki who was the *yojimbō,* or bodyguard, to the Sasagawa family. Hirate Miki is the popular person in the narrative of *Tempō Suikoden* who 'makes the blood flow at the Tonegawa dry riverbed'. Hirate Miki made a dramatic fight to the death as the samurai blades flashed in the moonlight. The overall purpose of the raid failed when they did not succeed in capturing Shigezō. This action is known to the world as the 'quarrel in the dry riverbed of the great Tonegawa'. Perhaps by virtue of it being so inconclusive, the battle set both sides at odds, until matters were resolved three years later when assassins from the Iioka side murdered Shigezō. This was a murder so underhand that even their own side did not admire the action, but it brought peace to the area.

Fire-fighting in Edo
The prevention and control of fires was one of the daimyō's most solemn obligations. For a daimyō to allow a fire to start in his own *yashiki* was an act of gross negligence. Here a daimyō's retainer, dressed in a fire-cloak and helmet, supervises operations.

The 'Battle of the Firemen'

The other demanding area of a daimyō's civil authority was the prevention and control of fires. Nowhere was this need more pressing than in Edo itself, and there was a considerable responsibility placed upon the daimyō owners of *yashiki*. If a daimyō allowed a fire to start within his *yashiki*, he was punished by a number of days confinement to his *yashiki*, but if the fire had not spread to other mansions, the punishment might not be carried out. Certain *yashiki* belonging to daimyō above 10,000 *koku* were allowed to have a look-out tower, the *hinomi*. The *hinomi* had mounted on it a bell and a striking-beam. Between 1704 and 1711, when orders were issued for the formation of fire brigades in Edo, the newly appointed commanders of the brigades, of *hatamoto* rank, were given leave to build *hinomi* 9 m (30 ft) high. There is the record of a certain Matsudaira samurai who 'having been charged, in the year 1810, with certain duties as to fires, he for the first time hung up a bell and a striking-beam, and during his term of office made use of the same'. Fire was of course an ever-present hazard in a city built largely of wood, and would spread so rapidly through it that if a fire started near Edo gaol, the prisoners were released on parole, with heavy fines if they did not return once the fire had been brought under control.

During the 250 years of the Edo Period, there were twenty large fires and three large earthquakes in the capital. In the fire of 1657, half the city was destroyed and over 100,000 people lost their lives. In 1772, half the city was again lost, and in 1806 nearly all the retainers' *yashiki* were swept

An earthquake
Earthquakes have always been a fact of life for the Japanese. Three major earthquakes hit Edo during the two and a half centuries of the Tokugawa. This rather poor-quality illustration from the *Gempei Seisu-ki* shows the effects of a tremor, which brings buildings crashing to the ground. The startled citizens run for cover.

away. The fire brigades were organised in a similar way to the *yoriki* and the *dōshin* who kept order in the city. They wore protective clothing made of leather and heavy cotton, and helmets similar to 'battledress' helmets, but with a cloak attached at the rear which buttoned under the chin. Cutting fire-breaks was the most effective means of controlling a blaze, and there are a number of exuberant wood-block prints which depict the firemen in action, using hooks to pull burning shingles off roofs (thatch was forbidden, for obvious reasons), and carrying buckets. Standing his ground, in the most visible position he dare occupy, is to be found the squad's standard-bearer. During the 1760s, water pumps were introduced and, with increased training, many potentially dangerous fires were averted.

There was, however, intense rivalry between the *hikeshi*, the fire brigades, which on one occasion erupted into serious violence. The greatest jealousy occurred between the members of the Edo *machi-hikeshi*, the 'city fire brigade', and the *daimyō hikeshi*, the brigades maintained by the individual daimyō in the city. The rivalry, which has great echoes of the violence between the *hatamoto-yakko* and the *machi-yakko*, probably had similar social origins, and the leader of the Edo *machi-hikeshi*, Shimmon no Tatsugorō, had the popularity and the airs of Banzuin Chōbe'e. He lived from 1800 until 1876, a time when memories of previous conflagrations made the citizens very frightened of the danger of fire, and ready to greet a successful fire-chief as the nineteenth-century equivalent of a conquering daimyō.

Tatsugorō's collision with the *daimyō hikeshi* took place with the fire brigade of the Arima daimyō of Chikugo. One night, Tatsugorō's *machi-*

The 'Battle of the Firemen'
One of the most extraordinary conflicts to have taken place in the streets of Edo was the battle between firemen of the Edo citizenry, the *machi-hikeshi*, and firemen of the Arima daimyō. At the end of the brief but violent argument, 18 men lay dead.

A water garden
A harassed daimyō, beset by the many duties which required his attention, would refresh his spirit by the contemplation of a garden, such as this beautiful example at a Zen temple in Okazaki.

hikeshi arrived at the scene of a fire to find the Arima brigade's standard flying over the scene. Tempers exploded, and the scene of the fire became one of carnage as the two groups of firemen attacked one another with their short swords and their fire-axes. By the time order had been restored, 18 men lay dead, a death toll higher than many of the celebrated vengeance feuds that scarred contemporary Japan. Tatsugorō took full responsibility for the lack of control among his men, and surrendered himself to the *machi-bugyō*. His resulting banishment was only temporary, and he was to end his life as personal retainer to the last of the Tokugawa Shōguns, Yoshinobu, during the civil war of the Meiji Restoration. He accompanied the doomed Shōgun during his flight from the imperial forces, and eventually died peacefully at the age of 75, as honoured as any warlord.

This was the world outside the samurai class which the daimyō was required to control, a world occupied by corrupt samurai, hereditary policemen, proud firemen, gambling bosses and bitter gangland feuds. The Edo Period may not have been scarred by the wars of the Sengoku era, but it can hardly be called an age of peace.

101

Sex and the Samurai

The great houses of daimyō of the Edo Period came into being by various means. Some were won, like the Hōjō, and then, unlike the Hōjō, were retained. Others were increased in the great shake-up after Sekigahara, or were created daimyō by the Tokugawa Shōgun. Yet, whichever way the houses were created, all shared the same desire – to found a dynasty that would carry the family name forward into the future, a noble name forged in the heat of battle, and made even nobler in the wisdom and virtue of successive generations of good government in peace-time. That was the ideal to which they all aspired, but the reality was to be that the maintenance of an honourable name was every bit as difficult in the age of peace as it had been in war. In wartime, daimyō houses could be wiped out in dramatic battles, but peace placed its own demands on behaviour, and sometimes these were more difficult to cope with. As well as the external pressures from administration and the suppression of crime, so much depended upon internal personal factors, upon the daimyō himself, upon his wife and concubines, and upon the quality of those who came after him.

A doll for the Boys' Festival
This display, set out in the living quarters of a temple in Kawachi-Nagano, for 'Boys' Festival Day' illustrates the value still placed on Japan's samurai past, and also reminds us that Japanese aesthetics are not always governed by restraint.

Two actresses from the Toei-Uzumasa Film Studios in Kyōto pose for the camera. They are wearing *kimono*, and their wigs are characteristic of the hair-styles of the eighteenth century.

Women and the daimyō

The relation of parent and child is limited to this life on earth; that between husband and wife continues into the after-life; that between lord and retainer continues into the life after that again.

This pious statement was quoted earlier as an illustration of the firm bond of loyalty between daimyō and vassal. We may now turn it on its head and examine its implications for the role of women in samurai society.

Women occupy a shadowy position in accounts of the Sengoku Period. When a woman comes into prominence, she is frequently cast either as an out-and-out villain or as a mere token, a pawn in a daimyō's game of power. There is no equivalent in the Sengoku Period for the only 'female warrior' in the whole of samurai history – Tomoe Gozen, wife of the Minamoto general Kiso Yoshinaka, who fought beside her husband in the campaigns of the Gempei War and met her death with him in 1184. Nor is there any woman remotely approaching the status of Masako, widow of the first Shōgun Minamoto Yoritomo, whom history presents as a bitter schemer, determined to destroy the Minamoto succession in favour of her own clan, the Hōjō.

In contrast, the daimyō of the Sengoku Period tended to use women as chattels, as objects who were useful for acquiring power through the device of *seiryaku kekkon*, the political marriage. So useful was marriage as a weapon that the making of political marriages was specifically banned on the rise to power of the Shōgun Tokugawa Ieyasu. In my *Samurai Warriors*, there is a description of the incredibly complex web of marriage alliances that linked the families of Takeda, Hōjō and Imagawa in the mid-sixteenth century; but it is to the more powerful daimyō that we must look to see how cynically marriage, or rather divorce, could be manipulated for political ends.

When Oda Nobunaga made his alliance with Tokugawa Ieyasu in 1561, following the Battle of Okehazama, he married his daughter to Ieyasu's son Nobuyasu. The girl fully understood that she was expected to act as a spy on her new family, which she did very successfully, and informed Nobunaga about a plot to kill him and replace him with Nobuyasu. The plot had been hatched, apparently, by her new mother-in-law. As the alliance with Nobunaga was very important to him, Tokugawa Ieyasu showed his good faith to Nobunaga by putting to death his son Nobuyasu and also his scheming wife.

Such channels of information could also be used for false intelligence. Oda Nobunaga was himself married to the daughter of his rival, Saitō Dōsan (1494–1556), and told his wife, quite falsely, that he was plotting with some of Dōsan's senior retainers to have Dōsan murdered. His wife dutifully conveyed the message to Dōsan, who obligingly put to death some of his most loyal men, greatly weakening his position against

A raid on a house
The women of a household flee in terror as a castle falls, and the enemy samurai gain access to their living quarters.

104

Nobunaga. It is not surprising that the wisdom of the age, enshrined in documents such as the *kakun,* or 'house-laws' of the daimyō, contained references to the dangers of trusting a woman, of which the most telling is one attributed to Takeda Shingen: 'Even when husband and wife are alone together, he should never forget his dagger.'

But no example of the political manipulation of women can quite compare with Nobunaga's use of his sister O-ichi, and her daughters. She was first married to Shibata Katsuie, Nobunaga's most senior retainer, but Nobunaga desperately needed a marriage alliance with the Asai family of Ōmi, so O-ichi was divorced from Katsuie and married to Asai Nagamasa, the heir of the family, in 1568. The alliance did not hold, and Nobunaga went to war against the Asai clan in 1570. When Nobunaga burned Nagamasa's castle of Odani in 1573, Nagamasa and his father committed suicide, having first returned O-ichi and her three daughters to Nobunaga. Nobunaga thereupon made O-ichi remarry her former husband, Shibata Katsuie.

In 1582, Nobunaga was murdered, and Shibata Katsuie led the opposition to a take-over of Nobunaga's domains by another of his generals, Toyotomi Hideyoshi. After his defeat at Shizugatake in 1583, Katsuie was besieged in his castle by Hideyoshi and he committed suicide, along with O-ichi. The daughters were again spared, and the victor, Hideyoshi, took the eldest as his wife.

This girl led the most unbelievably tragic life. She had already seen her father, mother and stepfather commit suicide and then be consumed by flames in blazing castles, and so much more was in store for her. As the Lady Yodo-gimi, the title she acquired on her marriage to the future dictator of Japan, she bore him a son, Hideyori, who was to inherit the whole of Japan as his kingdom at the age of 5, when Hideyoshi died in madness. Hideyori's succession was disputed by the newly victorious Shōgun Tokugawa Ieyasu, and in 1615 his heavy cannon bombarded Ōsaka castle, where the desperate Hideyori had taken refuge with his army, accompanied by the Lady Yodo-gimi. As Ōsaka castle fell, she too committed suicide, along with her son, as another Japanese fortress blazed around her.

The faithful wife

Nevertheless, in spite of being used in so many cynical ways, a wife was expected to show the same loyalty to her husband as he would towards his

---

A family commits suicide

The reader may recognise the inspiraton for this plate as being the dramatic scene in Kurosawa's film *Ran,* where the defeated warlord's family commit suicide in the blazing castle keep. A samurai wife was expected to show loyalty to her husband every bit as great as the loyalty he showed towards his lord. Hence such an act of mass suicide.

Two women are stabbing each other at the same moment, while in the background a man commits *seppuku,* assisted by a faithful retainer.

An understanding of the various motivations possible behind a decision to commit suicide is fundamental to an appreciation of *bushidō,* the code of conduct and honour of a samurai. The act of suicide could simply be one way of making a dramatic protest against

the conduct of one's lord. Alternatively it provided a means of 'wiping the slate clean' when one had failed, thus dying with honour. There are many examples of this from the battlefields of the sixteenth century. In the case of the family in this plate, the suicide is motivated by a desire to accompany the defeated lord in death, and serve no other master.

warlord. 'A woman has no specific daimyō,' said a moral tome of the period, 'she looks on her husband as her lord', a neat summary of the actual status of woman in feudal society. On the question of adultery, there was one rule for a man, and another for a woman. The 'house-laws' of the Tokugawa family made the right of a husband to kill an adulterous wife and her partner into a duty every bit as solemn as the duty of vengeance for a slain master.

There was, however, no such thing as adultery on the part of a husband, provided that another man's wife was not involved. The taking of concubines was no more than a means of ensuring that a daimyō house would produce a son to inherit, and the more concubines, the greater the chances of success. One daimyō, Mito Mitsukuni, of a branch family of the Tokugawa, who was known for his virtue, had assigned his inheritance to his brother's son, and, although he kept many concubines, obliged each one to undergo abortion lest the production of an heir should imperil his nephew's chances. Even in less extreme cases than this, the concubine was vastly inferior to the wife in a feudal household, having a rank of no more than a servant. Not that an unmarried daughter was much better off. She hardly ranked as a relative within the blood-line, her only function being to marry and beget children for her husband.

The lowest point to which samurai society brought women was the selling into prostitution of daughters and sisters, often from impoverished farming families. Although this practice was virtually unknown and for-

Yoshiwara – the pleasure quarter of Edo
This 'street' at the Toei-Uzumasa Film Studios in Kyōto gives one a good impression of the notorious Yoshiwara, the pleasure quarter of Edo. The prostitutes would ply their trade from behind the wooden, slatted windows that opened on to the street.

bidden in the Kamakura Period, which ended in 1333, the urbanisation of the Edo Period, and deteriorating agricultural conditions, ensured a growing demand and a steady supply. The story of the revenge of the sisters Miyagino and Shinobu, recounted later in this book, has as its background the selling of daughters into the brothels of Edo.

The Tokugawa Shōguns took a very pragmatic view of prostitution, much as they did towards the *kabuki* theatre, that it was a necessary evil but needed regulating lest it get out of hand. It, therefore, set up 'pleasure quarters' in the great cities, of which the best known was Yoshiwara in Edo. The name, literally, meant 'the plain of the reeds', but had a pun in its pronunciation which made it also sound like 'lucky field', not that the district itself had much luck. It was founded in 1617, and suffered four disastrous fires during the following two decades. The inhabitants of Yoshiwara: the girls, the pimps, the brothel-keepers and the clients, form the raw material of half the romantic literature, the plays and the wood-block prints of the Edo Period. A man taking his pleasure in Yoshiwara could, if he chose, bankrupt himself with the highest-ranking girls – the *tayū*, each of whom had the right to refuse any customer she did not fancy – or merely enjoy a little 'window-shopping' along the narrow streets, where the girls of lower grades would sit behind wooden slatted grills on the ground floor of the houses.

Comrade loves of the samurai

It is impossible to leave the subject of the personal relationships of the samurai class without some reference to the practice of homosexuality. Indeed, the attachment of men for men could in many cases far surpass the love of women, though bisexuality was as common as homosexuality. Takeda Shingen, for example, who produced many children through wives and concubines, had a particular attachment for his retainer, Kōsaka Danjō Masanobu. The devoted Masanobu became one of his most trusted, and most skilled, military commanders, and was instrumental in saving Shingen from defeat at the cataclysmic fourth Battle of Kawanakajima in 1561. It was, however, left to a novelist from the merchant class, Ihara Saikaku, who was born in 1642, to put into words the homosexual nature of much of samurai society. His writings, tongue in cheek as they were for many observations of his supposed betters in the world of Edo Japan, tease the samurai, as in one preface when he writes, 'Our eyes are soiled by the soft haunches and scarlet petticoats of women. These female beauties are good for nothing save to give pleasure to old men in lands where there is not a good-looking boy.'

Such attachments were not merely tolerated, they were encouraged, in what was predominantly a male society, as being conducive to comrade-ship and self-sacrifice on the battlefield. A young boy, taken into the service of a daimyō as a page, could almost expect to be used as an object of sexual gratification. For some retainers, to be the favoured page of a member of the lord's family was a gateway to further advancement. Others were forced to manipulate this position when a patron's interest waned, as in the case of Ōtsuki Denzō, whose success caused a split within the Maeda family.

Popular history, as represented particularly by the plays of the *kabuki*

Kōsaka Danjō, the lover of Shingen
In a predominantly male society, homosexual attachments could be stronger than those of marriage. Kosaka Danjō Masanobu was the lover of Takeda Shingen, and his constant companion. His prompt action at the fourth Battle of Kawanakajima in 1561 almost certainly saved the Takeda from annihilation. This photograph is of actor Hiroaki Murakami, who played the part of Danjō in the 1988 television series, 'Takeda Shingen', and is reproduced by kind permission of NHK Television.

A boy of the samurai class
This young actor from the Toei-Uzumasa Film Studios is dressed in simple fashion. His hair is tied back in a queue, without the shaven front portion which would later denote his entry into manhood.

大月傳蔵

一勇國芳

Ōtsuki Denzō

Ōtsuki Denzō has been treated unfairly as the epitome of villainy in the *kabuki* theatre. He was, in fact, a wise retainer, and suffered from the jealousy engendered in the other retainers by Maeda Yoshinori's affection for him, for which he eventually paid with his life.

theatre, has not dealt kindly with Ōtsuki Denzō. Of all the villains who enter the stage in a family feud, he is the epitome of treachery – the Japanese equivalent, one may say, of Shakespeare's caricature of Richard III. Denzō was born the son of an insignificant retainer of the Kaga-han, called Ōtsuki Shichiemon, and when he was 14, on account of his good looks, he was summoned by Maeda Yoshinori, and employed as his page with a considerable stipend of 2 ryō of gold. Denzō became very well acquainted with Yoshinori, being a very handsome youth, and the affection Yoshinori showered on him rivalled that given to the favourite children of the family.

Realising his good fortune, Denzō aimed at the chance of a successful career in the administration of the *han*. However, Denzō had not been born into the family's line, and it was made clear to him that he would be most unlikely to succeed to a position of responsibility once Yoshinori's homo-

Kanazawa castle
Kanazawa castle was the seat of the Maeda daimyō, and the scene of the epic feud between Ōtsuki Denzō and Maeda Naomi, immortalised, and much embellished, in the 'soap operas' of the *kabuki* theatre. The outer wall and gateway are all that remain of the castle, which is now the site of Kanazawa University.

sexual preference for him began to wane. In fact, he rose to a high position within the family, and the mere existence of the stories that have grown up about Denzō's machinations tell us a great deal about the jealousies that could be aroused within a family.

According to the 'treachery' theory, Denzō devised a cunning, but very risky, plot. He stole a poisonous plant from the *han* medicinal herb garden, and poured it into Yoshinori's bowl of soup. At the very instant when Yoshinori was about to put it into his mouth, Denzō shouted 'My lord! Wait a moment' and, making it appear he was loyal, drank from the bowl. As soon as he had the taste of poison in his mouth, he vomited copiously and fell in convulsions. Yoshinori was enormously impressed by Denzō's acute awareness of danger and his outstanding loyalty, and promptly increased his stipend by 1000 *koku*, and appointed him to a senior rank. He became entrusted with Yoshinori's personal affairs, acting as a go-between for his feudal lord with beautiful women, and even though these stories are embellished, they give a good indication of the services a retainer was expected to perform for a daimyō, particularly an idle one.

Denzō's greatest coup came in procuring for Yoshinori, as a concubine, a celebrated beauty called O-tei. She was Yoshinori's second concubine, and inevitably provided a rival to his existing paramour, O-kiku, a situation exacerbated when both became pregnant at the same time. Eventually both gave birth, O-kiku producing Yoshinori's second son, O-tei his third. In reality, though, O-tei was to insist, her son had been born two days

113

earlier, while the other child's birth was the first to be notified. This had serious consequences for them both, because should Yoshinori's eldest son meet with an early death, then the third son would rank as subject to the heir. Ōtsuki Denzō took up her case.

Soon after, Yoshinori took a new concubine. O-tei was distraught, and entered into a plot with Denzō to have Yoshinori and his heir murdered, as a result of which Denzō would have undisputed power within the clan. The story goes on to relate how Yoshinori is ambushed while returning from Edo on the *sankin kōtai* visit, and stabbed as his horse is crossing a flooded river. His heir, Munetoki, is poisoned, and the servant girl, who is made a convenient scapegoat, meets a horrible end in a pit full of snakes, one of the most bizarre scenes in all the *kabuki* repertoire! Denzō is eventually found out and exiled to a distant place, where he commits suicide.

Historical reality is much more sober, but in its way far more tragic. Denzō did succeed to a high position within the Maeda family as a result of Yoshinori's attachment to him, and it is true that on Yoshinori's death, which was from natural causes, he was exiled to Gokayama in Etchū province and killed himself in 1745. Why should this have come about?

Needless to say the other retainers, and the family members in particular, were violently jealous of Denzō, in particular a certain Maeda Tosa-no-kami Naomi, who was a pillar of society, and his branch of the Maeda family counted as first among the eight families of Kaga. Naomi, who had a burning sense of duty towards great affairs of the family, was an exemplary player at power politics. History also tells us that Maeda Yoshinori was not a careless ruler, nor was Ōtsuki Denzō a bad, scheming person, but one who stimulated and enforced economy among the retainers, and raised funds by borrowing gold from Ōsaka merchants. He handled difficult economic affairs of the *han*, not by oppression, but from a position of wisdom and strength. Yet the whole affair shows how fragile such a position could be. Once Yoshinori was gone, Denzō could be removed by jealous family members. To a daimyō, family blood was thicker than water, and, inevitably, as a counter to Denzō's personification of evil in the *kabuki*, the indignant Maeda Naomi is presented as a shining example of the loyal samurai.

The servant girl in the pit of snakes
This illustration, which is taken from a nineteenth-century, wood-block-printed book cover, summarises the *kabuki* plot as the 'soap opera' of its day. The scene, rarely performed nowadays, is the bizarre climax of a play based loosely on the events of the Maeda family feud.

The divided sword

The universal acceptance of concubines may have ensured the birth of an heir, but numerous offspring could lead to rivalry within a family as bitter as the mistrust between Maeda Naomi and the outsider Denzō. Yet even though the wars of medieval Japan were civil wars, there are very few examples of families being split over allegiance in wartime, such as happened during the English Civil War. Such a split did in fact happen to the Sanada family, which greatly imperilled their future; yet it was the loyalty between them, and their recognition of samurai duty, that saved the Sanada as a daimyō family.

The Sanada were a family of Shinano province. The first to bear the name, Yukitaka, submitted to Takeda Shingen when he invaded Shinano. He went on to serve him together with his elder son, Nobutsuna, who was killed in 1575 at Nagashino. His younger son, Masayuki (1544–1608), inherited his father's position and, on the ruin of the Takeda with the death

Interior of the Sanada mansion
The simplicity of the Japanese domestic interior was a common thread that united all classes. From the simplest home to a grand house such as this, the Sanada mansion in Matsushiro, the straw *tatami* mats and the unpainted wood were characteristic of a deep and meaningful unity.

of Katsuyori in 1582, he was one of many Takeda retainers who were made to submit to Tokugawa Ieyasu. Masayuki grew to have little love for the Tokugawa. As a result of Masayuki's submission to Ieyasu, his elder son, Nobuyuki (1566–1658), was taken as a hostage to Hamamatsu, and eventually married the daughter of Ieyasu's great captain, Honda Tadakatsu; but Ieyasu went much further in his demands on the Sanada, and in 1586 tried to strip him of his territory to give to the Hōjō. So Masayuki rebelled, in spite of his son's presence with Ieyasu. The Tokugawa army advanced on Ueda and laid siege to the castle, but a truce was patched up, owing to the intervention of Hideyoshi.

When war came again in 1600, Masayuki instructed his son Nobuyuki to join Ieyasu, as that was where his duty lay. For Masayuki, and the other celebrated member of the family, Yukimura (1570–1615), their duty lay in opposing the rise of the Tokugawa. (Their emotional parting has long been a favourite theme for Japanese artists.) Ueda castle was strategically situated on the Tokugawa's most vital line of communication – the Nakasendō road, and as it had already withstood one siege by the Tokugawa army, Masayuki no doubt thought it could withstand another. The Sanada family, thereupon, contributed to the Sekigahara campaign by delaying the progress westwards of Ieyasu's son, Tokugawa Hidetada, which they did so successfully that the siege of Ueda in 1600 is regarded as one of the three classic sieges of Japanese history when the defenders were

115

not defeated. A huge army was kept from Sekigahara, and had it not been for the attendant treachery on the field, their tactics may well have tipped the balance against the Tokugawa.

After Sekigahara, Masayuki and Yukimura were captured by the Tokugawa and faced almost certain death, but Nobuyuki interceded on their behalf and the sentences were commuted to exile. Nobuyuki was granted the castle of Ueda. Masayuki died in exile in 1608, and Yukimura returned from exile in 1614 to join the army that opposed Ieyasu once again from within the walls of Ōsaka castle. Here he was one of the most skilled of the defenders, and was finally killed in the Battle of Tennōji in 1615.

There seem to have been no bitter feelings from Masayuki to his son or vice versa. Each followed his duty as they saw it, and Nobuyuki carried on the family line, which to all of them was what really mattered. Through him the Sanada continued and prospered, and in 1622 he was transferred to Matsushiro, where they established the magnificent mansion which exists to this day.

A puppet from the Bunraku theatre
Like the *kabuki*, the plays of the puppet theatre would take their plots from contemporary events, such as family feuds. In fact the puppet plays tended to be more daring in their attempts at satire.

The Date family feud

The split within the Sanada family, mutually agreed by all parties as being in keeping with samurai honour and duty, is as nothing compared to the mighty rifts torn through the fabric of family loyalty in other great families, and there are several examples of daimyō families brought to the brink of ruin by corruption and feuding within their own blood-relatives. Unfortunately, as we have seen in the illustration of the Maeda family dispute, in the majority of cases, the facts behind these family feuds have been obscured by the treatment they received at the hands of novelists and dramatists, who used real-life stories of weakness and disaster among the rich and powerful as material for the 'soap operas' of their day. An excellent example is the near-disastrous rift within the Date family, daimyō of Sendai. The truth of the conflict is interesting enough as an example of the decline of loyalty and filial values, but the resulting story has been expanded out of all proportion.

Date Masamune (1566–1636) was one of the noblest daimyō to make the transition between Sengoku warlord and Edo daimyō, and the internal discord of the Date family arose entirely from the immorality of his grandson, the third generation daimyō Tsunamune. He devoted himself entirely to pleasure, with daily attendance in the red-light district of Yoshiwara. He was eventually condemned by the *bakufu*, an unusual and

A scene from **kabuki**
A wood-block print depicting a squabble between women of a daimyō's household. The scene is taken from the *kabuki* play *Meiboku Sendai Hagi*, which dramatises the events of the Date family feud.

117

very serious step for the Government to take, and as a punishment was made to underwrite the expense of the extension to the moat of Edo castle in 1660, an enormous civil-engineering project. But long before matters came to this pass, his retainers forced him to take early retirement in favour of his heir Kamechiyo (the future Tsunamura), who was still in his infancy.

The 2-year-old Kamechiyo's guardians were to be Date Hyōbu Munekatsu and Tamura Ukyō. Hyōbu was the tenth son of the *han* founder, Date Masamune, and Ukyō was Tsunemune's illegitimate elder brother. But Hyōbu Munekatsu was ambitious, and by and by clawed his way to absolute power, shielded from criticism by his relationship, through his son's marriage, to a powerful *bakufu* official. He dismissed senior retainers who opposed him, and promoted his particular favourite, a man called Harada Kai. Tamura Ukyō was gradually squeezed out of any control over the affairs of the *han*. In the 10 years of Hyōbu's office as guardian, he managed 120 retainers, and during that time had ordered 17 of them to commit suicide.

The story of the Date family feud forms the basis of the *kabuki* play *Meiboku Sendai Hagi*, which begins to diverge from reality at the point when Date Hyōbu is believed to have been plotting to murder the young heir, Kamechiyo, so that he could take over the domain. The child's nurse, Masaoka, tries to protect the boy by retiring to an inner room on the pretext of the child's illness. Two 'villains', acting on behalf of Date Hyōbu, bring cakes as gifts for the supposed invalid. The cakes are, of course(!) poisoned, and as a fine gesture of loyalty toward an infant lord, Masaoka's own son takes one to test it for poison. To avoid discovery of the fact that the cakes are poisoned, one of the villains stabs the boy to death.

In reality, the show-down with Hyōbu came from the person who was the next most powerful man in the family – one Date Aki Muneshige. The confrontation between Hyōbu and Aki made the Date feud grow more and more violent. Aki lodged a complaint with the *bakufu*, although he had little firm evidence on which to base his argument. Was there any more to the affair than Hyōbu's apparent incorrect treatment of land distribution? Aki stuck his neck out, and exposed fully Hyōbu's evil deeds and immoral acts as he saw them, accusations that forced the *bakufu* to intervene. The resulting investigation of Hyōbu's conduct and management took place in 1671 on neutral ground, at the residence of Sakai Ude-no-kami, the *tairō*, or chief retainer of the family, and therefore the most influential man outside the actual family.

Four people were questioned in turn about Date Hyōbu Munekatsu's conduct: Date Aki Muneshige, the retainers Shibata Geki and Yoshiuchi Shima, and Harada Kai. The accounts of the first three agreed totally, while Harada Kai's version differed wildly. Suddenly the investigation reached an unexpected climax when the enraged Harada Kai drew a short *wakizashi* sword and attacked Muneshige. Muneshige sustained two sword strokes and was severely wounded. The two other witnesses, Geki and Shima, chased after Harada and wounded him. Harada Kai was panting for breath, then lost his head completely and slashed indiscriminately at Geki and another retainer, called Haraya Yoshihiro, wounding them so badly that they died that evening.

But this sudden eruption into violence marked the end of the Date feud. Date Hyōbu Munekatsu's defence collapsed, and punishment was swift.

Harada Kai, villain of the Date feud
Harada Kai is the real-life villain
of the feud within the Date family
of Sendai. Here he is shown
brandishing a blood stained knife at
the residence of Sakai Ude-no-kami,
where his fellow conspirator, Date
Hyōbu, was impeached by the
bakufu for mismanagement of the
han.

The young heir, Tsunamura, was judged to have played no part in the
upheaval of the *han*, and to have been powerless to prevent it on account
of his youth. The *han* was, therefore, spared the confiscation by the *bakufu*
of its wealth, which totalled 620,000 *koku*. As for Date Hyōbu Munekatsu,
he was deprived of his stipend of 30,000 *koku*, and placed in the custody of
the *han*. He was reduced to an insignificant rank, and died eight years later,
in 1679, at the age of 51.

In the *kabuki* plays, Date Hyōbu Munekatsu and Harada Kai are the villains, while Date Aki Muneshige is presented as the finest of loyal family

members. However, this is in itself something of an exaggeration to make the play interesting. In reality, there was always factional strife among the loyal retainers of a large *han*, and to paint the combatants so clearly black or white is an oversimplification. The murderous outburst by Harada Kai, however, did actually happen, and is such a dramatic touch that one wonders why *Meiboku Sendai Hagi* has to be embellished so much, as, for example, in one scene when a sorcerer is introduced who changes magically into a rat!

Youth showing the characteristic pigtail and the half-shaven head, as modelled by an actor from the Toei-Uzumasa Film Studios in Kyōto.

The Kuroda feud

As a final illustration, let us examine the feud within the Kuroda family, which has received little embellishment. In this case, the dying lord, the great Kuroda Nagamasa (1568–1623), veteran of many battles including the invasion of Korea, hesitated before making his son Tadayuki his successor. There was much immorality in Tadayuki, Nagamasa reasoned, and he relied on his trusted *tairō*, Kuriyama Daizen, to remonstrate with him, even at the risk of his life. Nagamasa handed Daizen his famous helmet with water-buffalo horns and said, 'If Tadayuki gets foolish, put this helmet on and admonish him yourself.'

Legend says that Tadayuki had a favourite, Kurahashi Shudayu, whom he had originally procured as his personal retainer, and Tadayuki's

120

debauchery continued in spite of Daizen's remonstrations against him. Shudayu, another bisexual, procured a beautiful girl called O-hide no kata for Tadayuki, who was carrying Shudayu's child in her womb, through whom he was planning to usurp the family. However, evil did not prosper and O-hide no kata was killed by a retainer. In disgust, the *tairō* Daizen left the service of Tadayuki and lodged a complaint with the *bakufu*. Daizen had Tadayuki placed in the temporary custody of the Nambu clan and Kurahashi Shudayu was exiled to Toishima. The *bakufu* recognised the loyal service to the Tokugawa of the previous head Nagamasa, and maintained intact the territory of the Kuroda, to which Tadayuki was later restored.

That is the tradition, but how much is true? There was a show-down between the two men, Tadayuki and Daizen, and the model of Shudayu is said to be a person called Kuraya Sodayu, who existed as Tadayuki's professional flatterer, but the Kuroda feud is just one more story of a fight between a stupid ruler and a stubborn old retainer, a feature common enough to the turbulent world of the warlords of Japan.

Death and the Daimyō

The nearness of death, and the awareness of the nature of the spirit world, was an omnipresent factor in the life of the warlord. We have noted twice already that the relationship between daimyō and retainer was regarded as extending beyond death, and that terrible gap between life and death was one that every samurai had to be willing to cross. If loyalty meant anything, it had to include dying for one's lord. Many years after wars had ceased, a samurai of the Nabeshima daimyō was to put this principle into words: 'The Way of the Samurai,' he wrote, 'is found in death.'

The supreme sacrifice

The 'way of the Samurai' was found in death, and this death could be brought about by an enemy sword, spear or bow, or even a gun – the means did not matter as long as the death was honourable, and for a death to be honourable it had to come about as a result of loyal service to one's lord.

Suicide on the battlefield
The daimyō's loyal samurai hold off the enemy while their master commits *seppuku*.

The loyal exploits of Sengoku Hidehisa
Death in battle was the ultimate expression of a warrior's loyalty, and on occasions was actively sought, but such self-sacrifice did not always lead to the daimyō's advantage. Here the hero Sengoku Hidehisa (1551–1614) performs valiantly, in a companion scroll to that depicted on the cover of *Battles of the Samurai* by this author. (Ueda castle museum)

In times of war, the achievement of such a death was prized as the ultimate proof of loyalty, and on occasions death could actively be sought for its own sake. There is a very fine dividing line between accepting the likelihood of death in reckless battle and actively seeking it out, which was effectively to commit suicide. An appreciation of the place of suicide in the concept of the loyal samurai warrior is essential for understanding the many acts of seemingly wasteful self-destruction we read of in the old war chronicles. What motivated this apparent eagerness for extinction, and how could destroying oneself ever be seen as loyal behaviour?

There were occasions when suicide was regarded as appropriate because of failure, and the samurai would commit *sokotsu-shi*, or 'expiatory suicide', the very act itself wiping the slate clean. Such a decision could be spontaneous and dramatic, like the action of the veteran warrior Yamamoto Kansuke at the fourth Battle of Kawanakajima in 1561. As Takeda Shingen's *gun-bugyō*, he had devised 'Operation Woodpecker', by which the Takeda were to surprise the Uesugi army. Realising his bold strategy had failed, Kansuke took his spear and plunged into the midst of the enemy army, committing suicide to make amends for his error. Minutes after Kansuke's suicide, he was joined in death by Morozumi Masakiyo, Shingen's 87-year-old great-uncle mentioned earlier. To Morozumi, a dramatic suicide was a way of dying honourably when faced with what he interpreted as certain defeat. In his case, there was no sense of personal failure, merely the culmination of loyalty in joining Shingen in his coming death. The tragedy of both these deaths is that their interpretations of the certainty of the destruction of the Takeda very soon proved incorrect. Reinforcements arrived, the army rallied, and a defeat was turned into

123

victory. Yet two experienced generals had been lost, both of whom would have served Shingen better by staying alive.

The motivation behind suicide is much less well appreciated than the means whereby it was carried out, which was usually the well-known act of *seppuku*. (If the two characters which make up the work *seppuku* are reversed, it produces *hara-kiri*, the word more familiar to Western ears.) *Seppuku*, which has been much described and much discussed, was a particularly painful act of suicide in that the samurai himself released his spirit from its seat in the abdomen by a swift and deep cut with his dagger. The rite was somewhat modified in later years to allow the presence of a second, who cut off the victim's head at the moment of agony.

The committing of *seppuku* was not always a voluntary activity. It could be allowed as an honourable alternative to execution for a condemned criminal of the samurai class, and we also noted earlier how Sasa Narimasa was 'invited' to commit suicide by Hideyoshi following his disastrous

Seppuku *on the battlefield*
This page from the *Hōjō Godai-ki* shows the act of *seppuku*, or ritual suicide, at its most poignant and dramatic – the mass suicide of a defeated army. One warrior receives the blessing of a second to cut off his head. Others discard their armour for the classic act of *hara-kiri*, while one throws himself on to his sword.

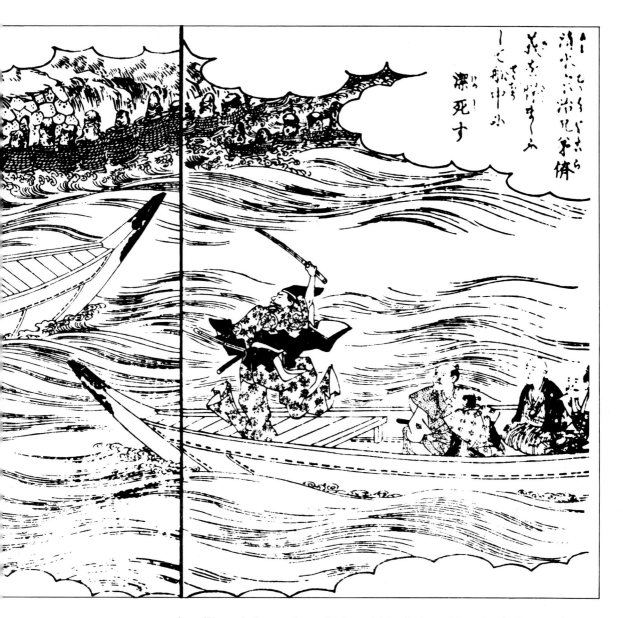

清水長左衛門宗治 花を惜しみ身を捨て舟中小 しく船中小 深死す

The suicide of Shimizu Muneharu
One of the most dramatic acts of suicide in samurai history was that of the defender of Takamatsu castle, Shimizu Muneharu, who took a boat out into the artificial lake created by Hideyoshi's siege operations, and committed *seppuku* in front of the besieging army.

handling of the territory Hideyoshi had given him. Sometimes a daimyō was called upon to perform *seppuku* as the basis of peace negotiations, the idea being that the surrender of a castle could be accepted without further bloodshed, providing that the current daimyō committed suicide. This would so weaken the defeated clan that resistance would effectively cease. Toyotomi Hideyoshi used an enemy's suicide in this way on several occasions, of which the most dramatic, in that it effectively ended a dynasty of daimyō forever, is what happened when the Hōjō were defeated at Odawara in 1590. Hideyoshi insisted on the suicide of the retired daimyō, Hōjō Ujimasa, and the exile of his son Ujinao. With one sweep of a sword, the most powerful daimyō family in the east ceased to exist, and disappeared from history.

Alternatively, the victor could be satisfied with the death of his enemy's

125

retainer, which would be most effective if the subordinate was in charge of the castle he was besieging. There are several examples of this from Hideyoshi's earlier campaigns on behalf of Oda Nobunaga. The most theatrical occurred when Hideyoshi besieged Takamatsu castle in 1582. It was a long siege, and only looked like being successful when Hideyoshi diverted a river to make a lake, which gradually began to flood the castle. Unfortunately it was during these operations that Hideyoshi received the dramatic news of the murder of Nobunaga, and knew that he had to abandon Takamatsu rapidly before any other of Nobunaga's generals found out and became his avengers instead. He hurriedly drew up peace terms with Mōri Terumoto, which included the clause that the valiant defender of Takamatsu, Shimizu Muneharu, should commit suicide. Shimizu Muneharu was determined to go to his death as dramatically as he had lived, and took a boat out into the middle of the artificial lake. When he was satisfied that Hideyoshi's men were taking careful note of what he was doing, he committed *seppuku*.

Sometimes such a suicide provided an honourable end only after extreme privations. Tottori castle, in Inaba province, held out for an incredible 200 days before it surrendered to Hideyoshi in 1581. Its commander, Kikkawa Tsuneie, inspired his men to this long resistance even though they were reduced to eating grass and dead horses. Tsuneie's suicide letter to his son survives to this day. It reads:

We have endured for over two hundred days. We now have no provisions left. It is my belief that by giving up my life I will help my garrison. There is nothing greater than the honour of our family. I wish our soldiers to hear of the circumstances of my death.

His suicide, along with that of two others, was the condition of surrender.

Another reason for committing suicide was the making of a protest. This is known as *kanshi*. Examples of this are rare, but it profoundly affected one of the greatest daimyō of the Sengoku Period. Oda Nobunaga inherited his father's domains at the age of 15 and, although he was a brave warrior, showed little interest in the administration of his territory. One of his best retainers, Hirade Kiyohide, tried in vain to persuade him to mend his ways, and when the young Nobunaga showed no inclination to listen to him, Kiyohide put all his feelings into a letter to his lord, and committed *seppuku* in protest. Nobunaga was greatly moved, and changed his ways for the better, with, of course, considerable consequences for the history of Japan.

Following in death

To return briefly to Shimizu Muneharu and his *seppuku* in the middle of the lake, there is a related anecdote which illustrates the one reason for committing suicide which did not meet with universal approval. This was the practice of *junshi*, or 'following in death'. In Muneharu's case, the loyal retainer actually preceded his lord in death, because Muneharu was invited to the man's room in Takamatsu castle the evening before his own suicide was due to take place. There his loyal retainer explained that, to reassure his master about the ease with which *seppuku* could be performed, he had himself committed suicide, and, pulling aside his robe, showed

秀吉の神祭
大宮父子が
害心を識く
害心を識く
殺さーむ

The execution of prisoners
One reason for the continuing tradition of *seppuku* was the fact that prisoners were invariably executed. The other alternative, to become a vassal of the victor, was often less palatable.

Muneharu his severed abdomen. Muneharu was touched by the gesture, and acted as his retainer's second to bring the act to a speedy and less painful conclusion.

As noted above, there was a fine line between *junshi* and merely continuing a desperate fight. In the confusion of a battlefield, the circumstances of a retainer's death could never be clearly established. But when death from natural causes during times of peace provoked the performance of *junshi*, whereby a loyal retainer committed suicide to show that he could serve none other than his departed lord, it could only be regarded as utterly wasteful. During the Sengoku Period, such an act may have been approved of, and indeed some retainers did have little left to live for, but in times of peace *junshi* was a deliberate, premeditated and unnecessary act, noble, perhaps, in its sentiments, but scarcely helpful in maintaining the stability of a dynasty.

In the early Edo Period, as many as 20 leading retainers of an individual daimyō were known to have committed *junshi* on the deaths of their lords. For this reason, strong condemnation was made of *junshi*. A better way to serve one's departed lord, the *bakufu* argued, was to render equally loyal service to his heir. But *junshi* was firmly engrained in the Japanese mentality. It had been abolished originally by an imperial decree in the year AD 3 (!), yet still the tradition persisted, and as noted above, reached its peak in the Sengoku Period. A strong condemnation of it is found in the so-called 'Legacy of Ieyasu', the 'house-laws' left by the first Tokugawa Shōgun in

1616, but at the death of his grandson, the third Tokugawa Shōgun Iemitsu in 1651, five of the leading retainers of the Tokugawa committed *junshi*, a remarkable gesture against the law they themselves had formulated. A further attempt to ban it was introduced by the *bakufu* in 1663, and included the statement:

In the event that a lord had a presentiment that a certain vassal is liable to immolate himself, he should admonish him strongly against it during his lifetime. If he fails to do so, it shall be counted as his fault. His heir will not escape appropriate punishment.

Five years later, an instance of *junshi* occurred among the retainers of the recently deceased daimyō of the house of Okudaira, but little action was taken against the family because of the great service the Okudaira had rendered to the Tokugawa in previous years. (Their ancestor had been the defender of Nagashino castle at the time of the famous battle there.) The family of the actual performer of *junshi* was not so fortunate. His two sons were ordered to commit *seppuku*, and his two sons-in-law, one of whom was of the Okudaira family, were exiled.

Other daimyō finally took note, and from the mid-seventeenth century onwards, the practice of *junshi* effectively ceased, until it came dramatically to the attention of modern Japan in 1912. On the eve of the funeral of Emperor Meiji, General Nogi and his wife committed *seppuku*. Nogi had commanded troops in the Sino-Japanese War of 1894–95, and led the battle to take Port Arthur in the Russo-Japanese War of 1904–05. It was an

A Buddhist priest at prayer
A Buddhist priest of the Shingon sect kneels in prayer at the temple of Fudō-ji, on the site of the Battle of Kurikara.

act that astounded his contemporaries because of the bizarre disloyalty to the Emperor's wishes that the illegal act implied. It was also sobering evidence that the samurai spirit lived on in the Japan of the twentieth century.

The death of an enemy

In the Sengoku Period, the death of one's enemy was the aim, and the natural consequence, of the practice of war. Nevertheless, the recognition of an enemy death became surrounded by considerable ritual, of which the most bizarre, to Western eyes, were the practices surrounding the collection and inspection of heads. This is a feature found throughout samurai history, and was the surviving element of the ancient practice of sacrifice to the gods of war mentioned in a previous chapter. The heads would be washed, the hair combed, and the resulting trophy made presentable by cosmetics – all tasks performed with great delicacy by the women of the daimyō's court. The heads would then be mounted on a spiked wooden board, with labels for identification. If the ceremony were to be held with no time for this preparation, the heads could be presented on an opened war-fan, or on a paper handkerchief. Some leaves from a tree were recommended to soak up any dripping blood. The daimyō would sit in similar state to the one he had enjoyed when he had presided over the departure ceremony, and one by one the heads would be brought before him for comment. If a daimyō were otherwise engaged, the head ceremony could be delegated to a trusted subordinate, as in the *Hōjō Go-daiki*:

It is Nakayama Shurisuke that Hōjō Ujitsuna favours with [the right] to raise the flags and sit on the camp-stool at Kōnodai. This is a person who is known for his traditional virtues of military lore and loyalty by which he has destroyed enemies, carrying out strategy in numerous battles, and at the same time he is a samurai official. This person will be bugyō *for head inspection. He will record the relative importance of loyalties, and examine the details of contests when the heads were taken.*

Of course, not all the hundreds of heads taken during a battle were saved. The *Gunyōki* quotes the following document:

Tembun 2nd year (1533) 7th month, 6th day at the Hour of the Monkey. The list for [the Battle of] Ōyama. These are the heads that were taken:

Item: one head:	*Maekawa Zaemon*
taken by	*Kinichi Danjōshū and Shōshu Uemon*
Item: one head:	*no given name known*
taken by	*a* chūgen *[called] Genroku*
Item: one head:	*Arakami Jirozaemon*
taken by	*Nagao Gagaku Sukeshu and Masuda Danjochu*

The number of heads taken and discarded is not known.

One little-known feature of the head-inspection routine was that certain expressions on the faces of the deceased were supposed to be unlucky, and others lucky, namely:

1   *Eyes looking towards heaven – unlucky (and particularly disliked by the Takeda family).*
2   *Eyes looking towards the earth – generally lucky.*
3   *Eyes looking towards the head's left – lucky in enemies.*
4   *Eyes looking towards the right – lucky in allies.*
5   *Eyes closed – lucky, 'a head of tranquillity'.*
6   *One eye closed, gnashing teeth, etc. – unlucky.*

The mention of the heads of allies above refers to the practice of sending back to an enemy the heads of their noble dead.

A special privilege was reserved for the head of a defeated enemy general or a daimyō. It would be brought before the daimyō by two men, not just one, and, after the victorious army had given the shout of victory, the general would ceremoniously eat the same three dishes of which he had partaken before setting out, but with a difference – the head of the defeated general was allowed to share the *saké*. In a grisly ritual, some *kombu* (dried seaweed) was placed in the head's mouth, and *saké* poured on to it, with much dignity, from a long-handled cup.

As may be imagined, the expression on the face of a dead daimyō was very closely examined, as the chronicle *Ō-monogatari* tells us of the occasion when Oda Nobunaga viewed the head of his bitter enemy, Takeda Katsuyori, in 1582:

When Oda Nobunaga inspected the head of Takeda Katsuyori the right eye was

Oda Nobunaga views the heads
One of Oda Nobunaga's retainers is overcome by emotion as he contemplates the severed head of an enemy, during one of Nobunaga's head-viewing ceremonies following a victory.

130

closed and the left eye was enlivened with a scowl. Nobunaga was moved to sympathy at the sight of the dead head of the powerful general, and it is recorded that all concerned agreed that Nobunaga may have been victorious in battle, but had been defeated by Katsuyori's head.

The Japanese spirit world

The attitude of a samurai towards his own death, and that of his family, lord and enemy, was deeply coloured by his beliefs regarding the world of the spirits of the dead, to which the act of dying committed him. The religious beliefs of the Japanese relating to death and dying are not easy for non-Japanese to appreciate, as was brought home to the world's media in 1985 when the then Japanese Prime Minister Nakasone made an official visit to the Yasukuni Shrine in Tōkyō on 15 August, the fortieth anniversary of the end of World War II. There was considerable protest from overseas, particularly from the Chinese, who pointed out that war

The Mimakude Shrine
The Mimakude Shrine, where are enshrined the spirits of the Kusunoki family, is typical of thousands of such Shintō shrines throughout Japan. Note the characteristic *torii* gateway.

criminals, such as General Tōjō, were enshrined there. Analogies were drawn with President Reagan's equally unpopular visit to the West German military ceremony at Bitburg, where the remains of SS troops were buried. But there the resemblance ended. Bitburg contained human remains, while Yasukuni contained nothing at all – and there we have the key to understanding the notion of the Japanese spirit world.

A Shintō shrine, like Yasukuni, is neither a burial ground, nor is it simply a place of worship, like a Christian church, a synagogue or a mosque. It is also a spirit house, a gathering place for the spirits of the dead enshrined there. Since ancient times, the Japanese have believed that the spirit lives on after the death of a body, returning from time to time to the land of the living. The season of cherry blossoms is one of these times, when the *tama* (spirits) flock to the cherry-tree-covered hills of Yoshino. The midsummer festival of *Bon* is another occasion on which the spirits of the dead are welcomed back from the mountains or other sacred places where they live. In many parts of Japan, lanterns are floated on water to light the spirits' way home. In this Shintō scheme, the worlds of the dead and the living are coterminous. The spirits of the dead are always close at hand, and the theme of communication between the living and the dead is a strong theme running through Japanese tradition.

Shintō is, of course, not the only religion of Japan but, being so thor-

A Buddhist grave
A large stone *sotoba* marks the site of a Buddhist grave, where the cremated remains of a samurai are buried. Buddhism teaches that the soul is reborn after death in a state of reincarnation.

The Buddha of mercy and the vengeful judge
Two aspects of Buddhist cosmology are illustrated here. On one hand there is the beatific figure of the healing Buddha, Amida, who waits to welcome souls into his Western Paradise. On the other is one of the fierce judges of the underworld, whose judgement will decide into which of the states of transmigration the reincarnated soul will be born.

oughly grounded in traditional beliefs and folk practices, it has managed to absorb much of other religions within its own world view, so that even though the influence of Buddhism (introduced during the sixth century AD) encouraged the custom of preserving the ashes of the dead in family graves, the spirit has always been regarded as more important than the body. In most aspects of religious life, Shintō and Buddhism can be regarded as totally intermingled until the Separation Edict of 1868, which sought to make Shintō an 'Established Church'.

Sharing this acceptance of two apparently contradictory religions, the samurai believed that, 33 years after death, a person's spirit moved from the Buddhist temple where he or she was buried to a shrine, an idea totally contrary to the Buddhist doctrine of reincarnation, which saw the spirit existing in limbo, waiting to be reborn, and we read comments made to a dying samurai like, 'May you be reborn in bliss'.

This process of rebirth was not without its hazards. Where a spirit ended up depended on the person's actions during his life, and no one else's prayers made the slightest difference. There was a very strong belief in judgement during the sixteenth century. People believed that the Ten Kings of the Underworld, in Buddhist cosmology, passed judgement on each person's spirit after death. Seven days after death, the spirit was judged by King Shinkō; seven days later it was judged by King Shokō, and so on every seventh day until on the forty-ninth day, seven weeks after death, the verdict was handed down and the spirit was reborn in one of the six realms of transmigration – hell, the realm of Hungry Ghosts, the realm of the Beasts, the realm of the Asuras, or Titans, the human realm, or heaven. Above these six realms were the four states of enlightenment leading to final Buddhahood – the *sravaka*, the *prateya-buddha*, the *bodhissatva*, and finally, the completely enlightened *nirvana*. The spirit's individual 'case' was reviewed after a hundred days, a year, and three years. During the Tokugawa Period, the Buddhist memorial period for the dead was stretched from 3 years to 7, 13 and 17 years, until, finally, 33 years was accepted as the time of trial.

Shintō shrines were the homes for these spirits, and it is noticeable from old chronicles that the daimyō of the Sengoku Period would honour the fallen impartially, enshrining the spirits of friend and enemy alike. The act of enshrinement was very important, because it was believed that any-

The temple of Daitsu-ji, Nagahama
The Daitsu-ji is a large Buddhist foundation at Nagahama. Buddhism and Shintō are the two major religions of Japan, and have much in common. We are looking at the *hondō*, or main hall.

134

Parade of yamabushi
Yamabushi from the Shōgō-In in Kyōto march to their *goma* ritual.

one who had died unjustly or by violence, including on the battlefield, would become a *onryō*, or 'angry ghost', and haunt the living and cause misfortune. Even peaceful spirits at death could change their nature and become malevolent if neglected during the 33-year period. The samurai had a vivid concept of the nature of these unruly spirits. They saw the spirit right after death as having 'sharp edges'. If you enshrined it, it slowly lost its rough edges until it was 'as smooth as marble'. After the period of 33 years, these featureless spirits then gathered into one collective spirit – the 'god of the village'. Presumably the spirit of the war criminal General Tōjō is now 'as smooth as marble', owing to the safeguards of enshrining it

---

Yamabushi

This plate is an attempt to reconstruct the appearance of the members of the Shugendō sect, the *yamabushi*, as they would have appeared in the sixteenth century. They are on pilgrimage in the Yoshino mountains and are paying homage before a statue of Fudō. Fudō is always represented with a fierce expression and surrounded by flames. In his right hand he holds a sword to strike down demons, and in his left he holds a rope with which to bind them. The *yamabushi* themselves look unkempt, which is supported by contemporary descriptions of them, but they wear their traditional skull-cap and carry staffs. These, with the details of the robe, symbolise various aspects of Buddhist doctrine.

Successive pilgrimages such as these, which included performing rituals of prayer and fasting at ancient ly defined sites, were a form of initiation into the mysteries of Shugendō. *Yamabushi* were therefore regarded as the possessors of mystical powers. They were believed to be able to cast out demons, to talk to animals and to overcome fire. The sect was suppressed at the end of the nineteenth century, but has since undergone a revival, and annual pilgrimages are now undertaken.

correctly in 1978, 33 years after his death? Seen in this light, the existence of Yasukuni Shrine is not a glorification of the past, but a safeguard for the future.

However, a different Buddhist view of death was provided by the 'mass movement' Amidist sects that developed during the thirteenth century. According to the sect called Jōdo Shinshū, on death the believer's spirit left the world immediately for Amida's paradise, which explains the fanaticism of the *ikki* armies of the Sengoku Period, who vanquished daimyō forces, secure in their belief that death in battle ensured instant heaven. But even though such beliefs about the dead appear contradictory, they were regarded as complementary, and were firmly rooted in Japanese tradition. For example, the spirit of Taira Masakado, who was killed in AD 940, is enshrined in the Kanda Myōjin shrine in Tōkyō. Masakado was a rebel against the Emperor, and during the Meiji Period, when the institution of the Emperor was being strengthened against the memory of the overthrown Shōgun, it was decided to move Masakado's spirit from the main shrine to a subshrine. When this was done, local people refused to go to the main shrine, and boycotted its annual festival, the reason being, apparently, that it was wisest to keep an unruly spirit pacified, and that if Masakado's spirit was deprived of its proper shrine, then it would start causing trouble again.

Nagahama castle
A modern reconstruction of the keep of Nagahama castle, which was originally built for Toyotomi Hideyoshi.

The **yamabushi** *light the sacred bonfire*
The climax of the *yamabushi*'s *goma* is the lighting of a huge bonfire in the centre of the courtyard. Strips of wood, containing petitions, are flung into the billowing white smoke that ensues.

Communication with the spirit world

Although the living had a duty to perform to the recently dead, there were benefits to be gained from the departed spirits, who could pass the barrier between our world and theirs. The Japanese medium, or *miko*, allowed the spirit to possess his or her body, and transmitted messages to the living. Closely related to the *miko* was the notion of the ascetic who acquired special powers, the best known of whom were the *yamabushi*, the followers of the religious sect of Shugendō. *Yamabushi* means 'he who lies in the mountains', and the term has often been applied erroneously to the armies of warrior monks who plagued Kyōto during the twelfth century. Yoshitsune's companion, the warrior monk Benkei, disguised himself and his companions as *yamabushi* to avoid detection during their flight from Yoritomo's vengeance in 1185.

The figure of the wild-looking, wandering *yamabushi* is one that crops up regularly in Japanese art and literature, and we noted earlier how Hōjō Sōun recruited a *yamabushi* as his *horagai* blower. A *yamabushi* was endowed with magical powers, acquired as a result of fasting, onerous climbs of sacred mountains, and various ascetic exercises, such as standing naked under waterfalls. The initiate was believed to have the power to cast out demons, to talk to animals, and to overcome fire. By the recitation of prayers, *yamabushi* could overcome and exorcise any *onryō*, the above-mentioned 'angry ghosts', that were causing trouble in a locality.

The *yamabushi* thus reflected a blending of the Buddhist, Shintō and animistic traditions which were outlined above. To a *yamabushi*, a mountain was not just the abode of the *kami* (the gods of Shintō): it was a Buddhist mandala — a sacred space separated from ordinary space and time. His climb was a spiritual journey as well as a physical one, and the disciple passed symbolically through the ten worlds of transmigration. Each of these states was negotiated by means of a rite, the ordeal representing hell being vividly described during the sixteenth century by a former *yamabushi* who had become a Christian. The ritual, called *gōhyō*, or 'weighing one's karma', consisted of the disciple being tied and seated on a beam projecting over a cliff, with a large rock as a counterweight. In this terrifying position, he was required to confess his sins to his fellow *yamabushi*. If he confessed all, his karma was lightened. If he refused, he would be tipped off into the valley below. The rite of the Hungry Ghosts, which followed, was fasting; of the Beasts: abstinence from water; and of the Asuras: *sumō* wrestling. Following the final rite for heaven, a sacred dance, the climber received a form of baptism, confirming his powers as a *yamabushi*.

The rituals of the *yamabushi* lasted, with little change, right through the time of the samurai, but with some reduction in the severity of the disciplines. Shugendō all but ceased to exist with the Meiji Restoration, but has since been revived, and I was privileged to join some modern *yamabushi* on an ascent of their holy Mount Ōmine in 1986.

There are numerous references in war chronicles to daimyō consulting *yamabushi*, and more orthodox priests. It was, in fact, quite common for daimyō of the Sengoku Period to become monks while continuing the profession of warlord. Takeda Shingen and Uesugi Kenshin are the prime examples, and their banners with Buddhist prayers were among their most treasured possessions. Other daimyō took a more sceptical view of religion.

'Fearing neither gods nor Buddhas' is a frequent phrase used to describe such iconoclasts, as in the legend of 'Hideyoshi's Bridge':

On the sacred mountain of Kōya-san, where lie the mausoleums of numerous daimyō, there are three bridges on the road that leads to the tomb of the saint Kōbō Daishi. According to tradition, the third bridge cannot be crossed by anyone whose morals are unacceptable to Kōbō Daishi, and a sinful person could not proceed further. After Hideyoshi had risen to the highest position in the Empire he made a ceremonial pilgrimage to the tomb of Kōbō Daishi. Knowing that during his career he had committed many acts of violence, Hideyoshi went to the third bridge the night before and made a trial crossing. Nothing happened, and relieved of the anxiety that he would be publicly embarrassed Hideyoshi returned to the bridge the following day and marched over it in a grand and contemptuous manner.

The Duty of Vengeance

If the loyalty due from a retainer to his daimyō was tremendous in life, it became all the more so after his death. But whereas *junshi* remained condemned for the larger part of samurai history, there was an entirely opposite requirement for revenge. Should one's lord die as a result of murder or other foul play, then a retainer's revenge was his by right. In fact, it went far beyond a right: it was a solemn duty, both sanctioned and practised at the highest levels of the samurai class.

The rules of vengeance

The notion of vengeance is inseparable from the ideals of the noble samurai. To the samurai, a man who took revenge was a man of honour; while he who shrank from this obligation was beneath contempt: a person to be despised more than the villain who had performed the original deed for which vengeance was sought. Such sentiments appear throughout samurai history, from the revenge of the Soga brothers at the time of the first Shōgun Minamoto Yoritomo in the twelfth century, to the classic epic of the Forty-Seven Rōnin (recounted in detail by me in *Samurai Warriors*).

The story of the Forty-Seven Rōnin, although the best-known outside Japan of any story of revenge, is not typical. The details, briefly stated, are that Lord Asano was required to commit *seppuku* as punishment for the crime of drawing a weapon within the Shōgun's palace, and wounding the

The revenge of the Soga brothers
The duty of revenge was found throughout samurai history, as illustrated by this wood-block print from the author's collection, which depicts the revenge of the Soga brothers during the twelfth century.

The Forty-Seven Rōnin
In this detail from one of many prints produced on the subject of the Loyal Retainers of Ako, the avenging rōnin engage the retainers of Kira in a fierce swordfight.

official who has been taunting him. His retainers, who survived him, hatched an elaborate plot of revenge in complete secrecy, turning to drunkenness and debauchery as a cloak for their intentions,which were achieved in a spectacular raid. Having taken the head of their lord's 'judicial murderer', they surrendered to the authorities, and committed suicide.

There are, in fact, very few examples in Japanese history of the murder of a daimyō and his subsequent avenging. Indeed, the Forty-Seven Rōnin is the only example of revenge being carried out in peace-time at such an elevated social level. This uniqueness probably accounts, to some extent, for the enduring popularity of the tale. It is also atypical in the secrecy with which the deed was carried out, which thereby put the avengers outside the law, and in the resulting condemnation by the authorities. The point illustrated by the Forty-Seven Rōnin is that, although revenge was central

---

The Forty-Seven Rōnin

The exploit of the Forty-Seven loyal retainers of Ako is vividly brought to life by this plate. They have arrived outside the gate of Kira's mansion. A dog is silenced for the split second before the enormous mallet crashes against the timbers of the gate. Their leader, Ōishi Yoshio, despatches men to the rear of the house.

Ōishi Yoshio was a pupil of the *bushidō* theorist Yamaga Sokō, and this expression of the loyalty to one's master due from a samurai is the best known practical illustration of *bushidō* in Japanese history. Yet even this famous raid was not without its critics. Yamamoto Tsunetomo, the author of *Hagakure*, a classic of *bushidō* writing which begins with the words 'The Way of the Samurai is found in death', praised the act of revenge on the grounds that it was the conduct to be expected, but went on to question the means whereby it was carried out. Yamamoto Tsunetomo was an adherent of the Wang Yang Ming school of Confucian philosophy, which taught that knowledge should always be accompanied by action, action that was swift and immediate. The revenge of the Forty-Seven Rōnin had been long in the planning, and Tsunetomo expressed surprise that it took so long for them to act. Dramatic acts of revenge were what appealed to men of such opinions, not a calculated and secretive plot such as that of the gallant Forty-Seven.

to the samurai philosophy, it must not be presumed that in carrying out revenge, a man was entirely free to do as he liked. Certainly, by the eighteenth century, the procedure of revenge was very clearly recognised.

If a deed was committed which required avenging, the avenger was required first to present a complaint to the daimyō, from whom he would get authorisation to search for and slay the enemy. This authorisation would be in the form of a letter certifying his identity, and indicating the name of his own *han* and the purpose of his search. After this, if everything had been carried out in perfect order, the particular way in which he slew his enemy was of no consequence, providing it was not attended by public disorder. Once the deed was done, the avenger was required to report immediately to the nearest authorities and explain the circumstances of his revenge. He would be interrogated on the details by the *machi-bugyō*, and asked the name of his family and of his *han*. He would then be required to present satisfactory proof that he had in fact been authorised to carry out the deed. Once his revenge was acknowledged as accomplished according to the rules, he was released from custody and walked away a free man, as in the account of the vengeance of the great swordsman, Miyamoto Musashi:

Miyamoto having encountered his enemy on the way, struck him and killed him. Having revenged himself in that manner, he narrated what he had done to the

Swearing vengeance before the lord's head
Retainers of a dead lord kneel in reverence before his severed head, swearing vengeance on his killer. Vengeance was the samurai's privilege and solemn duty.

The Mountains of Iga
The misty Mountains of Iga shelter the town of Iga-Ueno, scene of the Igagoe Vendetta.

daimyō of the province, who instead of blaming him, congratulated him and sent him back in security to his lord's territory.

The duty of vengeance received its solemnest expression in the collection of laws and recommendations referred to as the 'Legacy of Ieyasu', attributed to the first Tokugawa Shōgun, who died in 1616. The section dealing with revenge is a later addition, but sums up beautifully the requirements of the vendetta:

In what is concerning the revenge to be exercised against the man who killed your father or lord, it is expressly written by Confucius that you and your enemy cannot live together under the same heaven.

In consequence of that, the man who has an act of revenge to do must first notify it to the Court of Criminal Justice, which must neither prevent him from accomplishing his desire, nor obstruct him in its execution. Whatever be the case, it is prohibited to kill his enemy by raising troubles or in a riot.

The individual who revenges himself without notifying it to the Court of Criminal Justice, must be considered as a wolf, and his punishment or pardon will depend on the circumstances.

The Igagoe Vendetta

Even though revenge for the death of a daimyō is a very rare event, there are, however, many examples where a daimyō was intimately concerned

147

with a blood feud among his own retainers. The best example of this is the Igagoe Vendetta, which we shall study in some detail, because of the illustration it provides of the legal requirements surrounding the vendetta which we have outlined above.

The city of Ueno lies about 97 km (60 miles) due east of Ōsaka, among the wooded mountains of Mie prefecture. It is commonly called 'Iga-Ueno' (Iga being the name of the pre-modern province of which Ueno was the provincial capital) to distinguish it from the better-known Ueno, which is a district of metropolitan Tōkyō. Nowadays, Iga-Ueno is a mecca for tourists interested in the famous *ninja*, bands of whom had their headquarters in these remote valleys; but this is a modern phenomenon, and for centuries Iga-Ueno was known for a very different reason: as the site of one of the most dramatic acts of vengeance in Japanese history – the Igagoe Vendetta.

The Igagoe Vendetta has its origin in the incident when a certain Watanabe Gendayū was murdered by Kawai Matagorō, a retainer of the Okayama *han*. The Okayama *han*, which was under the control of the Ikeda family, had for some time been troubled by dissension among the samurai retainers, and between the retainers and the daimyō. The murder of Gendayū, which was in a sense the culmination of these troubles, happened on the night of the lively *Bon Odori* festival in 1630 in Okayama, the castle town which was the *han* capital, hundreds of kilometres from Iga-Ueno on the shores of the Inland Sea. That night, Matagorō, accompanied by some companions, was visiting Kazuma, a retainer of his comrades. Kazuma's younger brother, Gendayū who was keeping him company, was absent at that precise moment. Somehow a brawl developed. Matagorō and his associates mortally wounded Gendayū and took flight. Gendayū died very shortly afterwards, while Kawai Matagorō ran away from Okayama and went to Edo.

At this point in the story, we note the involvement of the daimyō. Watanabe Kazuma, who now had the responsibility of avenging his brother, was only 16 years old, and at first seems to have hoped that the Ikeda daimyō would bring Matagorō to justice on his behalf. But relations within the *han* had become so strained that Matagorō was safe in Edo, where a comrade, called Andō Jiemon, eagerly sheltered him. Even the daimyō himself, Ikeda Tadao (1602–32), could not enter unannounced, but hoped that, by employing various stratagems, he could capture Kawai Matagorō, who had caused him a great deal of trouble in the past. A raid was, in fact, carried out, but was seriously bungled. The attackers overcame Andō Jiemon but let Matagorō escape.

Before long, Ikeda Tadao died of a disease, smarting from the humiliation caused him by this public evidence of dissension among the retainers. Such was his tenacity of purpose that his dying wish is supposed to have been: 'For my memorial service, above everything else offer on my behalf the head of Kawai Matagorō.' His younger brother, Ikeda Teruzumi (1603–63), took to heart his elder brother's dying wishes, and relations among the retainers, some of whom openly supported Matagorō, increasingly took a dangerous turn. The be-all and end-all was the existence of Watanabe Kazuma, who sought revenge, and whose unfulfilled desires acted as a goad.

Eventually, the *bakufu* stepped in and officially ordered the exile of Kawai Matagorō. As it was the Shōgun's orders, a samurai had to submit, and by this preserve the honour of the Okayama *han*. This was Kazuma's

Araki Mata'emon
Araki Mata'emon, a swordsman of the Yagyū Shinkage-ryū, became the hero of the Igagoe Vendetta when he helped his brother-in-law, Watanabe Kazuma, to track down and kill Kawai Matagorō.

opportunity. He was now 18 years old and able to save his own honour as well as that of the Okayama *han*, so he applied to the Ikeda family for discharge and, with official approval, began to search everywhere for Kawai Matagorō.

Kazuma left the service of the Ikeda family in the ninth month of 1832. At the end of much hardship and long journeying, he located Kawai Matagorō, in the eleventh month of 1834, in the neighbourhood of Iga-Ueno. By now Watanabe Kazuma had been joined in his revenge by his sister's husband, Araki Mata'emon, one of the foremost swordsmen of the day. We know that Araki Mata'emon was a swordsman of the celebrated school of fighting called the 'Yagyū Shinkage-ryū' and had been taught by Yagyū Mitsuyoshi. He served the Matsudaira family of Yamato-Koriyama and gave instruction in *kenjutsu*, and seems to have combined good intelligence with swordfighting skill, as related by an anecdote about Mata'emon fighting a swordsman called Yamada Shinryūkan. This Shinryūkan's favourite weapon was the *kusari-gama*, which consisted of a very sharp sickle, to the handle of which was attached a long weighted chain. The skill in using the *kusari-gama* was to whirl the chain at high speed, thus either keeping a swordsman at bay or entrapping his sword. The weight could also be spun to catch the opponent's leg and pull him over. When faced by this weapon, Araki Mata'emon enticed his enemy into a bamboo grove, where the *kusari-gama* could not be used effectively, and overcame him.

Sometime during the period of Kazuma's quest for revenge, Araki Mata'emon took his leave of the Matsudaira *han*, and volunteered his services as his brother-in-law's 'second'. The alliance caused great consternation among Matagorō and his followers, for one of their number had once been defeated by Mata'emon in a fencing match.

On the seventh day of the eleventh month of 1834, Watanabe Kazuma,

The Kagiya crossroads at Iga-Ueno
The scene of the Igagoe Vendetta is marked nowadays by this stone at the Kagiya crossroads in Iga-Ueno.

150

Araki Mata'emon and two others waited for Kawai Matagorō's faction in Iga-Ueno. They had been reliably informed that Kawai Matagorō was *en route* from Ōsaka to Ise, a journey that would take them through Iga-Ueno. That morning the road was frozen. At the Hour of the Dragon (8 am), Mata'emon and followers entered a shop belonging to a certain Yorozu Yakiemon at the Kagiya Crossroads in Iga-Ueno, and waited for Matagorō's party to arrive along the road from Ōsaka. One man of their party stood guard. The time passed very slowly. Apparently Matagorō's uncle, Kawai Jinzaemon, complained of a chill, and their pace had slackened, so they entered Iga town later than Mata'emon had anticipated.

In one of several novels written about the incident, Mata'emon's guard whispers 'They have come!', keeping his voice as low as possible. Mata'emon and his followers leave the shop and line up at the crossroads; then in a gesture towards samurai honour, Mata'emon returns alone to the shop to settle the account of one *sen*. No doubt this incident is included to show the great swordsman's attention to the mundane, and to demonstrate his desire not to be troubled by money during such a great affair. It is also a fact that by this gesture of honesty towards his host, thereby disregarding the chance of being killed within the next few minutes, he would show himself as a samurai who was a defender of the law. This was of crucial importance. The whole of the vendetta had to be carried out according to the spirit and the letter of the law.

The Igagoe Vendetta
A vigorous wood-block print depicting the vengeance of Watanabe Kazuma at Iga-Ueno.

The six-hour blood feud

The law prevailed right through the conflict that followed. Mata'emon first struck the old Jinzaemon, and also killed the followers who were surrounding Matagorō. (The story as it has grown puts the number slain by Mata'emon at 36). But Mata'emon had decided that he did not intend to kill Matagorō. Kazuma was the one to do that, as the law demanded, so Mata'emon pushed Matagorō to Kazuma's side. He himself patiently joined his companions and did not invite them to join in. The Igagoe Vendetta was, in essence, a duel between Kazuma and Matagorō, and nothing must inconvenience it, nor must there be unnecessary deaths.

The duel between Kazuma and Matagorō continued for six hours until the Hour of the Ram (2 pm). Both became so weakened in mind and body that they could not even see their opponent. Nevertheless Mata'emon did not intervene. In a hoarse voice, he encouraged Kazuma, and at one point was able to head off Matagorō from scaping. Discipline was also maintained by Matagorō's side, who had supported him during his exile. There was an equal need for their side to be seen to be behaving according to the law and the dictates of samurai honour. If Matagorō behaved in accordance with the wishes of the Emperor, he might regain the daimyō authority following a victory. So he made a desperate effort. Much more than samurai honour was at stake.

By now the sun was sinking in the west, and the area around the Kagiya crossroads was dotted with corpses, and only Kazuma and Matagorō's

The Erin-ji
The temple of repose of Takeda Shingen, one of the greatest of the Warlords of Japan, as seen from its magnificent garden.

violence could be heard. But a resolution of the combat was not far away. Kazuma hit home on Matagorō, and just before Matagorō responded, Kazuma's sword cut the artery in Matagorō's left arm. Half of Matagorō's body was dyed with blood, and as he fell Kazuma dealt him a decisive and final blow to the neck.

To the bitter end, the law had priority, and the duel at the Kagiya crossroads became famous as a legal duel, ending as it had begun. Mata'-emon and the others carried out the appropriate procedures afterwards, and surrendered themselves to the local Tōdō *han*. They had fulfilled the legal requirements to the very end. There was no riot, and Mata'emon and the others had not killed people indiscriminately. Their operation had been conducted within the limits laid down by law.

The Kameyama Vengeance

One important aspect of the Igagoe Vendetta is that the revenge killing was actually carried out by the immediate kin of the murdered man. Should this prove impossible – the passage of time, for example, preventing such an act from taking place – then the duty of revenge passed from that man to his son, and on, theoretically, until the final generation, when revenge could be gained. The outstanding example of this is the Kameyama Vendetta, which, unlike the Forty-Seven Rōnin and the Igagoe Vendetta, is virtually unknown outside Japan.

On the morning of the ninth day of the fifth month of 1701, beneath the

---

The flags of the Takeda family

In this plate are shown the flags of Takeda Shingen and those of his 'Twenty-Four Generals' of which details have survived.

They include the large standards of the Takeda family, passed from father to son (which are described in the text), the centipede flag of the messengers, Shingen's personal *uma-jirushi* of three 'flowery-edged' *mon*, and the flag with three *mon* which identified Shingen's personal retainers.

The blue flags of Anayama Baisetsu (d. 1582) (drawn to scale) illustrate the range of flags available to one of Shingen's generals. As Anayama is in the *shinrui-shū*, i.e. the 'relatives', the large *sashimono* worn by his mounted samurai and the smaller one worn by those on foot bear the Takeda *mon*. The long *nobori* and *uma-jirushi*, however, have the same coloured ground, but an individual device. The same would apply to the others of the 'Twenty-Four Generals' illustrated here who were family members, namely the two Takedas. Itagaki and

Ichijō. With the others we may assume that the device that appears on the *uma-jirushi* appears also on the *sashimono* and the *nobori*.

The other flags are the personal *uma-jirushi* of the 'Twenty-Four Generals'. As noted in the text, the term is not a contemporary one, nor were they all active over the same period. In some cases the colours of the flags are controversial. Reading from left to right:

Top row: Kōsaka Danjō Masanobu, Omari Torayasu (killed at Ueda, 1548), Takeda Nobukado (brother of Shingen; design also shown as black on white), Takeda Nobushige (killed at Kawanakajima 1561) and also his son Nobutoyo, Yamamoto Kansuke (killed at Kawanakajima 1561)

Second row: Tada Mitsuyori (d. 1563), Tsuchiya Masatsugu (killed at Nagashino 1575), Obu Toramasa ('red regiment', executed 1565), Obata Toramori (d. 1561), Okiyama Nobutomo (killed 1575)

Third row: Oyamada Nobushige, Sanada Yukitaka (d. 1574), Yokota

Takatoshi (killed 1550), Saigusa Moritomo (killed at Nagashino 1575), Obata Masamori (son of Toramori, d. 1582)

Fourth row: Ichijō Nobutatsu (Shingen's brother), Itagaki Nobukata (killed at Ueda 1548), Anayama Baisetsu, Hara Masatane (killed at Nagashino 1575), Sanada Nobutsuna (son of Yukitaka, killed at Nagashino 1575)

Fifth row: Yamagata Masakage (brother of Obu Toramasa, who inherited the 'red regiment', killed at Nagashino 1575), Naitō Masatoyo (killed at Nagashino 1575), Baba Nobuharu (killed at Nagashino 1575; alternative design has flag black on white, as shown in frontispiece), Hara Toratane (died 1564)

Not illustrated here are the flags of Takeda Katsuyori, Shingen's heir, who had two *uma-jirushi*, each bearing the character *ō* meaning 'great', one white on black, the other reversed, and Morozumi Masakiyo. whose flag was light blue with the family *mon*.

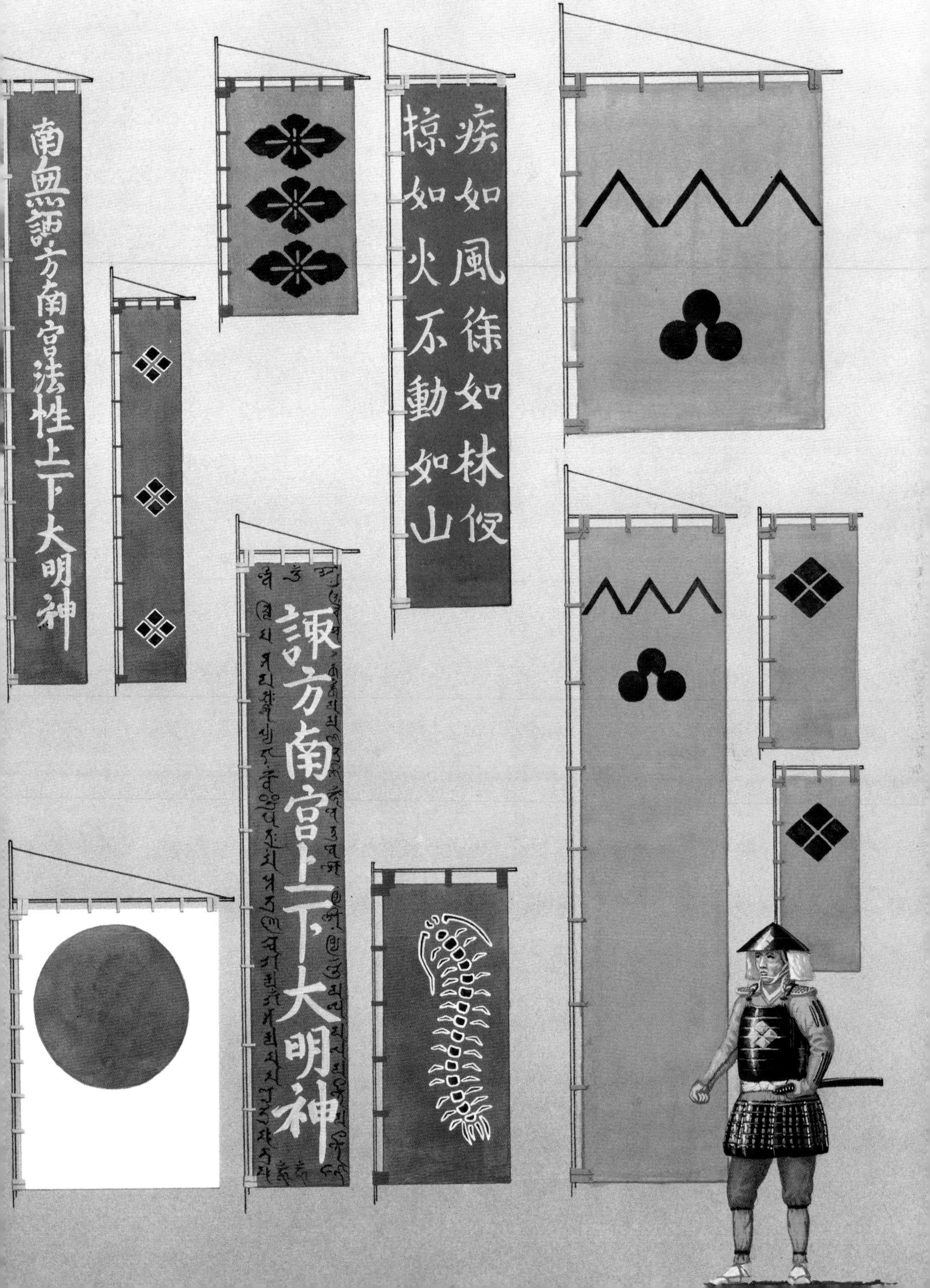
南無諏方南宮法性上下大明神
疾如風徐如林侵
掠如火不動如山
諏方南宮上下大明神

Ishigaki gate inside Kameyama castle, Akabori Sui-no-suke, a retainer of Itagaki Shigefuyu, the keeper of Kameyama castle, was heading for guard duty when his attendant heard the voices of two men, and a sword stroke was brought down from his forehead to his neck. As he fell, the two men gave him a finishing stroke. After this, they tied a message by a cord to Sui-no-suke's *hakama*, and departed calmly, the deed having been accomplished. Some retainers of the Kameyama *han* spotted them and chased after them, but the two men got away. According to the message, the two men who murdered Akabori Sui-no-suke were Morihei, a sandal bearer, and Hanemon, an attendant, and it became clear that they had killed the man who had killed their father. They had carried out this vengeance, they wrote, in accordance with the traditions of the samurai class, and after a wait of an amazing 28 years!

Their late father, one Ishii Uemon, was a samurai who received a stipend of 250 *koku* as a retainer of the keeper of Komoro castle, in Shinano. On the twenty-ninth day of the third month of 1662, his overlord agreed that he should become the warden of Ōsaka castle, and he moved to Ōsaka together with his four sons. This Uemon was a friend of a *rōnin* from Otsu in Ōmi province, called Akabori Yugen, and he was asked if Yugen's adopted son, Gengoemon, might come and study in Ōsaka. Uemon gave his whole-

Journey on the Nakasendō
To seek vengeance, a samurai would wander for years along the roads of Japan in search of his quarry.

156

hearted consent, and summoned Gengoemon to Ōsaka, on the understanding that he applied himself diligently to the martial arts.

However, this Gengoemon was an arrogant young man, and showed little progress in skill when he began instruction in spear fighting with the assembled pupils. On being reprimanded by Ishii, Gengoemon got very angry and challenged him to a contest. Ishii Uemon reluctantly agreed to a contest with wooden swords, but Gengoemon used a real spear, yet was easily defeated. As a result, Gengoemon lost face with his fellow pupils and, when the opportunity presented itself, he murdered Uemon and fled.

Uemon's son, Hyōemon, was 18 years old at the time, and personal retainer to the daimyō Munetoshi. That night he was on guard duty, and on learning of his father's death he applied for leave of absence, and set off in search of revenge. However, the enemy was nowhere to be seen. A long search began, and that winter Hyōemon killed Gengoemon's father Akabori Yūgen in Otsu, hoping thereby that Gengoemon would make an appearance; but he did not turn up. That act made Gengoemon also thirst for revenge for *his* father, and he tracked down Hyōemon to a bath house. Gengoemon attacked him suddenly from behind. Hyōemon drew his sword at the same time and thrust for his thigh, but a deep wound from the first swordstroke led to his death.

The defence of Chihaya castle
One of the most celebrated acts of defiance in samurai history was the defence of Chihaya castle by Kusunoki Masashige and his tiny army. In this section from a painted scroll, owned by the Nampian Kannon-ji at Kawachi-Nagano, the defenders set fire to a bridge.

Thereupon, the duty of revenge passed to his younger brother, and Uemon's second son, Hikoshichiro, set out on a quest for vengeance, but ill luck led to his early death. Two young children were left, who were being cared for by a relative called Aki. The third son, Genzō, was 6, and the fourth son, Hanzō, only 3. Gengoemon felt a sense of relief because the remaining sons were just young children, but a relative who was a retainer of Itagaki, the keeper of Kameyama castle, nevertheless recommended vigilance, and proposed that he should enter the service of the Itagaki. Gengoemon was given a stipend of 150 *koku*, and changed his name to Akabori.

Through Aki, Genzō and Hanzō nurtured their desire for revenge, and through him also heard of their enemy's change of name and that he had become a retainer at Kameyama. Genzō was not yet 14, but wanting to comply with the wishes of his family, he sent Aki on a quest for revenge. He came to Kameyama and sighted Sui-no-suke, but there was no way to sneak into the castle, and he spent an ineffective day. In 1688, the youngest son, Hanzō, became 17, and the brothers felt confident enough to take matters into their own hands. Leaving Aki behind, the two went to Edo, and studied the comings and goings of the Itagaki clan on the *sankin-kōtai*, disguised as pedlars. Then they got the chance to serve Hirai Zaiemon, a senior retainer of the Itagaki daimyō. At the time, when Zaiemon was to accompany his overlord on the *sankin-kōtai*, the two Ishii brothers went along as *chūgen*. No sooner had they begun to rejoice on being able to enter the castle than Zaiemon unfortunately died a natural death, and they saw their enemy departing for Edo, while they were unable to prevent it. However, their lowly service had at least brought them within the circle of the Itagaki retainers. Genzō changed his name to Morihei, and Hanzō to Hanemon, and impressed the *bugyō* by their soberness. Soon they grew to have the confidence of the castle family. The two frequently met and talked about their revenge, and as fellow retainers they kept watch on their enemy, Akabori Sui-no-suke.

Then came the day of realising their ambition. In the morning of the ninth day of the fifth month of 1701, at the Hour of the Dragon, 8 am, Akabori Sui-no-suke was making his way under the Ishigaki gate, accompanied by his sandal bearer. The brothers came up from behind and shouted simultaneously, 'We are the sons of Ishii Uemon, Genzō and Hanzō, and you are our father's enemy Akabori Gengoemon. Fair Play!' They cut him from forehead to neck. Sui-no-suke unsheathed at the same time, but the wound was too severe, and he fell. Sui-no-suke's sandal bearer fled. The two brothers tied the message to his *hakama*, fled from Kameyama and wrote a letter to their family, expressing satisfaction at the outcome. Then they went to Edo via the Nakasendō, and reported to the *machi-bugyō*, but neither received any punishment for their deed. Instead, because of the talent they had shown, they were enlisted by Aoyama Tadashige, keeper of Hamamatsu castle in Tōtōmi, and were each given a stipend of 250 *koku*.

The Revenge of the Daughters

Let us conclude this account of the duty of vengeance by noting that its requirements were by no means confined to the male line of a family. Once again, the most celebrated example is practically unknown outside Japan.

A woman's revenge
The duty of revenge was not confined to the male line of a family. On occasions, as shown by this illustration from the *Ehon-Taikō-ki*, a woman could revenge her lord in dramatic fashion.

The courtyard of the Keitoku-In
The site of the passing of the last of the Takeda warlords, Katsuyori, the Keitoku-In shows many characteristics of the styles of dwellings with which the daimyō would have been familiar.

This is the vengeance of the two daughters, Miyagino and Shinobu. Popular accounts of this affair exist in many versions. The *kabuki* play *Gotai eiki shiro ishi banashi* is the result of the joint work of three persons, and, like most *kabuki* plays, is much embellished, particularly with romantic detail.

The factual basis of the story concerns a samurai, called Shiga Daishichi, who was on the run because of a misdemeanor and hid in a paddy-field in a village near Shiro-ishi-banashi, in Mutsu. By chance, he was observed by a farmer, Yomosaku, who had been transplanting rice seedlings, and in his surprise Shiga Daishichi panicked and killed the farmer. Yomosaku had two daughters, the eldest of whom, Miyagino, had (according to the more romantic versions of the tale) been engaged to be married, but through poverty had been sold into prostitution and become a *tayū*, a courtesan of the highest status in Yoshiwara, in Edo. The younger daughter, Shinobu, intending to tell her elder sister about her father's death, went to Edo from far away, and, not being familiar with the topography, she was helped by a person at the Kaminari gate of Asakusa. By chance, he was the master, Muneteru of the Okurosha, where Miyagino was employed. Shinobu was taken by Muneteru to the Okurosha, where she was teased by the girls for her naïve provincialism. Her Mutsu accent revealed her to her sister, so the girls met, and Shinobu recounted their father's untimely last moments.

In the *kabuki* play, she says: 'The man who did it has been captured by our uncle the village headman.' Miyagino, too, when she knew of her father's death, said: 'Such an event brings my tears, . . . let us pray that our requests be granted. . .' The audience expresses sympathy at this scene, one of the great tear-jerkers of the *kabuki* stage. At all events, the two daughters, Miyagino and Shinobu, secretly slipped away from Yoshiwara in order to seek revenge for their father's death, and began to study the martial arts under the guidance of Miyagino's samurai fiancé. They were eager in their pursuit of knowledge, and the result was the vengeance on their father's enemy, Shiga Daishichi, in 1649.

The girls were determined to carry out the revenge themselves. When the time was ripe, they went through the formalities of asking their daimyō overlord for authorisation to avenge the death of their father. There was, in this case, no need for a long search for the enemy, as he had remained in the daimyō's service. The lord accordingly ordered him to be brought before him, and, according to the popular accounts, the girls set on him there and then. Miyagino was armed with a *naginata*, the long curve-bladed polearm which by the Edo Period had become the traditional weapon for women. Shinobu wielded a *kusari-gama*, the sharpened sickle to which was attached a long weighted chain. With the aid of the chain, Shiga Daishichi's sword was rendered ineffectual, and the other sister finished him off with her *naginata*.

This remarkable duel, carried out in front of the approving daimyō and his senior retainers, has proved a popular theme for wood-block prints. In the *kabuki* play *Shiro-ishi-banashi*, Miyagino is freed from servitude as a courtesan and is united with her fiancé, and lives happily ever after.

Exposure of heads
Wax dummies at the Toei-Uzumasa Film Studios remind us of the surest proof of a samurai's loyal service: to bring back the severed head of his enemy.

The end of vengeance

The above examples serve to illustrate how the notion and duty of revenge

Vengeance
This crude fragment from a *kawaraban*, or broadsheet, depicts a revenge killing, probably that of Miyagino and Shinobu. *Kawaraban* were the forerunners of modern Japanese newspapers, and often featured vendettas in their accounts of contemporary life.

was a feature of samurai culture from the earliest times. The Meiji Restoration dealt the death-blow to the tradition of samurai revenge, as it was to do to so many aspects of the warrior tradition. The imperial decree forbidding revenge was issued in February 1873, and went as follows:

Assassination being absolutely prohibited by the law of the Empire, the Government's duty is to punish any individual who kills another.

According to ancient habits, it was an obligation on a son or a younger brother to revenge a father or elder brother, nevertheless, personal interest must not lead one to transgress the law and despise the public powers by revenging himself. Whoever so acts cannot be pardoned, the more especially because in that case it is impossible to know who is in the right and who in the wrong. Therefore from this day, no one shall have the right to avenge or pass judgement for himself. If unfortunately someone has done wrong towards a member of your family, take your complaint and explanations to the authorities, but do not follow the ancient custom, or you will be punished according to law.

There were many more decrees to come: the abolition of the wearing of the pigtail, the restriction of the wearing of swords to the armed forces, and soon the actual abolition of the name and class of samurai itself; but of all the new laws that took Japan into the modern world, none so eloquently reversed the duties of a previous age, and set at nothing the values of the 'Warlords of Japan'.

161

APPENDIX I
The 1559 Hōjō Register

The typical daimyō's retainer band was commonly divided into three main parts, namely: family members and relatives (which might include others regarded as equivalent to family because of a long and close relationship); *fudai*, the hereditary retainers of the family; and 'outsiders', either the surviving retainers of conquered enemies, the inhabitants of newly gifted lands or simply newcomers whose loyalty had yet to be tested. Allied families were usually placed in this category. There is often a separate unit for the daimyō's bodyguard, but its members tended to be recruited from the *fudai*.

The balance of evidence seems to be that only the troops furnished by the 'family members' category bore the family *mon* on their *sashimono*. The *fudai* and allies fought under the flag of their commander, and the daimyō's bodyguard and messengers usually had their own distinctive appearance.

The Hōjō register, the *Odawara-shū shōryō yakuchō*, listed the military

The Hōjō bodyguard
A samurai wearing the *sashimono* of the personal guard to the head of the family.

The personal standards of the Hōjō family (not to scale)
Upper left: the Hōjō *mon* in black on a very large white banner of *shihō* type (horizontal dimension exceeds vertical), used by Hōjō Ujiyasu; *right*: a long inscription (practically untranslatable!) in black on white, used by Hōjō Ujimasa; *lower left*: 'hachiman' in black on pale yellow, used by Hōjō Tsunanari.

The character mu
The character *mu*, which means 'nothing', is a popular device in Japanese heraldry. It appears within a black ring on the *uma-jirushi* of Sengoku Hidehisa (1551–1614), and here as the *uma-jirushi* of Hōjō Ujinao (1562–1591). According to Takahashi, an identical banner was used as a *sashimono* by Uesugi Kenshin up to about 1555. He presented it to Usa Sadayuki, his general in charge of the messenger unit, following one of the Battles of Kawanakajima (probably the second, in 1555).

obligation of the retainers of the Hōjō in 1559, under the third daimyō Hōjō Ujiyasu. There would also be a sizeable contribution to the army from the daimyō lands, which were not registered. Each of the retainers counted below would have had to supply men in accordance with the current compilation, which gives roughly 10,000 men. (The notes are the present author's observation.)

Unit Name	Notes, and prominent members	No. of retainers
Gokamon	('relatives', inc. heir Ujimasa, 2nd son Ujiteru, 3rd son Ujikuni)	17
Go-umawari-shū	('the daimyō's bodyguard')	94
Takoku-shū	('allies')	28

Units identified by geographical location —

Tamanawa-shū	(inc. Hōjō Tsunanari, Ujiyasu's adopted brother)	18
Miura-shū	(inc. Ujiyasu's 4th son Hōjō Ujimitsu)	32
Kotsuke-shū	(inc. Ujiyasu's 5th son Ujihide, adopted by the Uesugi in 1563)	29
Tsukui-shū	(inc. Naitō family)	57
Izu-shū	(inc. Kasawara family)	29
Matsuyama-shū	(inc. Kano family)	15
Edo-shū	(inc. Toyama family)	103
Odawara-shū	(inc. Matsuda family)	34

Other units

Ashigaru-shū		20
Temple land		28
Shrine land		13
Shokunin-shū	(craftsmen)	26
Total retainers listed		560

APPENDIX II
The 1575 Uesugi Register

This list is particularly interesting as, in addition to similar information to that for the Hōjō in Appendix I, it shows the various weapons to be supplied. The totals, from 39 names of retainers (simply classified as *ichimon*, family; *fudai*, inner retainers; and *kuni-shū*, country units) are as follows:

Mounted samurai	600
Foot-soldiers	
Spearmen	4,899
Flag bearers	402
Arquebuses	360
Reserves (inc. servants etc.)	610
Grand total:	6,871

The fine detail shows how the above proportions of one mounted to ten foot-soldiers are maintained throughout the army. As examples, for the family (*ichimon*) and family equivalent (*kakushō*), they appear as:

Name	Spears	Reserve	Arquebuses	Flags	Horsemen	Total
Uesugi Kagekatsu	250	40	20	25	40	375
Nagao Kagetori	106	15	10	10	15	156
Nagao Kagenobu	54	10	4	5	8	81
Sambonji Sadanaga	50	10	2	3	6	71
Kamijō Masashige	63	15	2	6	10	96
Murakami Kunikiyo	170	20	25	15	20	250
From among the eleven fudai *families*						
Matsumoto	101	15	13	13	16	158
Honjō	150	30	15	15	30	240
Yamayoshi	235	40	20	30	52	377
Naoe	200	30	20	20	35	305

Name	Spears	Reserve	Arquebuses	Flags	Horsemen	Total
From the kunishū, *well-known names are:*						
Nakajō	80	20	10	15	15	140
Irobe	160	20	12	15	20	227
Takemata	67	10	5	6	10	98
Kakizaki	180	30	15	15	20	260
Saitō	153	20	10	12	18	213
Shibata	135	20	10	12	17	194
Yasuda	60	15	5	5	10	95
Shimojō	32	10	2	3	5	52
Shimazu	58	10	6	7	10	91

The proportions and the overall numbers are very similar to an earlier, but less detailed, Uesugi Register of 1559. Combining this with contemporary accounts of the Fourth Battle of Kawanakajima it is possible to reconstruct the divisions of the Uesugi army at this encounter. (See my *Battles of the Samurai* for a detailed account of the fighting).

Forward troops
Vanguard: Kakizaki, Shibata, Shimazu
Second rank: Suibara, Takemata, Saitō
Third rank: Suda, Matsumoto, Shimojō

Headquarters troops
Takanashi, Ōgawa, Ayukawa, Inoue, Murakami, Watauchi
Irobe (*gun-bugyō*), Usa (messengers)

Flanks
Right: Yamayoshi, Shibata, Kaji
Left: Nagao, Yasuda, Honjō

Rear-guard
Nakajō, Koshi, Ozaki

Support
Amakazu (who held the ford at Amenomiya), Naoe (supplies)

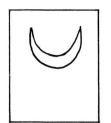  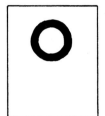 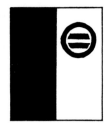

   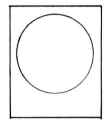

   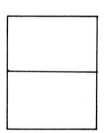

 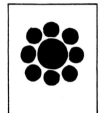  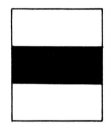

The personal standards of the Uesugi generals

Depicted here are the remaining known designs of flags used by Uesugi Kenshin's generals which are not shown elsewhere in the plates in this book. All are in black and white except where noted. Reading from left to right:

Top row: Suibara (white on red), Saitō, Takemata, Matsumoto

Second row: Nagao (dark blue on white), Yasuda, Usa, Irobe (red on white)

Third row: Yamayoshi (red disc, black inscription), Ayukawa, Inoue, Amakasu

Fourth row: Naoe, Nakajō (retainers' *sashimono*), Murakami, Sambonji (white over red)

APPENDIX III
Takeda Shingen

The following list is taken from the *Kōyō Gunkan*, showing the obligation to the Takeda Shingen by family, hereditary retainers and newly acquired vassals:

Name	No. of horsemen	Name	No. of horsemen
Family members			
Takeda Nobutoyo (son of Nobushige)	200	Ōyamada Nobushige	250
		Amari	100
Takeda Nobukado (brother of Shingen)	80	Kurihara	100
		Imafuku	70
Takeda Katsuyori (heir)	200	Tsuchiya	100
		Akiyama	50
Ichijō Nobutatsu (brother of Shingen)	200	Hara Masatane	120
		Ōyamada Bitchu no kami	70
Takeda Nobuzane (brother of Shingen, killed at Nagashino)	15	Atobe	300
		Others (four names in total)	255
Takeda Zaemon (cousin of Shingen)	100		
		Ashigaru taishō	
Nishina	100	30 names, commanding 255 horsemen, 785 *ashigaru* in all	
Mochizuki	60		
Katsurayama	120		
Itagaki Nobukata (killed at Ueda, 1548)	120	*Semposhū* (by province)	
Kiso	200	Shinano (includes Sanada family)	2020
Anayama Baisetsu	200		
		East Kozuke	1035
Fudai		Suruga	430
		Totomi	320
Baba	120	Hida	150
Naitō	250	Etchu	170
Yamagata	300	Musashi	180
Kōsaka	450		

Navy (41 ships, no numbers of crew given)

Shingen is also said to have had a bodyguard of 6,373, though whether these were drawn from the above or were his direct retainers is difficult to say. It seems a very large figure, even for such an important daimyō.

APPENDIX IV
Hashiba Hideyoshi

In 1573, following the defeat of the Asai family, Hashiba (later Toyotomi) Hideyoshi achieved a certain degree of independence from Oda Nobunaga by being granted in fief the castle of Nagahama. The details of his troops and their heraldry are interesting in providing a 'snapshot' of the future *Taikō* at one stage of his rise to glory. Unfortunately there are no numbers or weaponry given.

His *uma-jirushi* was a single golden gourd. Takahashi Ken'ichi, in his book *Hata Sashimono*, devotes several pages to a discussion of whether or not Hideyoshi ever did adopt the famous 'thousand-gourd standard', and notes that as late as 1575 only one gourd is to be seen. (This is on the famous painted screen of the Battle of Nagashino.)

His retainer band organisation follows the pattern common to many daimyō. There are the *ichimon-shū* (relatives), the *fudai-shū* and the *shinzan-shū* (literally 'newcomers'). This latter group is divided geographically by province, giving the Omi, Mino and Owari-*shū*, and includes such names as Ishida Mitsunari (Omi) and Yamauchi Kazutoyo (Owari).

The *fudai-shū* included a seven-man contingent who formed Hideyoshi's personal bodyguard known as the 'yellow *horō-shū*'. (Compare Nobunaga's use of black and red *horō* in his army.) Their numbers were later raised to 22.

Hideyoshi's messengers, 29 in all, were distinguished by an identical gold-coloured flag (see illustration).

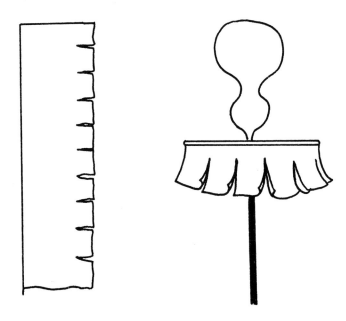

Hideyoshi's flags
These sketches illustrate the golden gourd standard, with its golden flag, and the style of flag used as a *sashimono* by Hideyoshi's messengers.

APPENDIX V
The Ii 'Red Devils'

The troops of Ii Naomasa and his son Naotaka, the most loyal of the Tokugawa *fudai*, formed an important part of the Tokugawa army at Sekigahara and at Ōsaka, and provide the most striking illustration of a *fudai* contingent adopting its own distinctive colours. The *Iika Gumpō*, quoted by Takahashi, gives the full regulations for the appearance of this army, to a degree of detail that is quite unique. Takahashi gives no date for the document, but it probably dates from the early seventeenth century.

Item, the standard is a 5-shaku [1 shaku = 1 foot] length of four widths of silk. On a red ground, the mon, *which is the character 'i' in gold in the centre. The pole is lacquered black.*

*Item, personal large banner [*nobori?*] is two widths of silk, 1 jō [9 feet] long. The* mon *on red ground. By invitation, on a 7-shaku length, on a red ground, the characters 'Hachiman Dai Bosatsu' in white. The pole is lacquered black.*

Item, the uma-jirushi *is a gold fly-catcher, with a black-lacquered pole.*

Item, mounted samurai, on a 5-shaku length of two widths of silk, on a red ground the surname written in gold.

Item, retainers' personal flags the same, excepting that by invitation the family mon *in white on a red ground.*

Item, ashigaru's *back-flags, three, each of one width of silk, 5 shaku long, immediate* ashigaru *a red field with no* mon, *retainers the* mon *of the family of birth in white.*

Item, armour, harness, saddle and stirrups to be red, with the exception that retainers may display in gold the mon *of their family of birth.*

Note how much the heraldry adopted depends on the nature of the relationship, such as being a retainer or a warrior directly commanded by the lord. The regulations fit almost exactly with the figures depicted on the painted screen depicting the Ii army at Ōsaka. Using a rule of thumb of two mounted and twenty foot-soldiers per 1,000 koku the Ii contingent at Ōsaka would have consisted of about 20 and 200 men respectively, plus their own followers. On the screen appear the 19 mounted samurai, of whom 9 wear red *horō*. There are 123 samurai on foot, mostly armed with long spears. Nearly all have inscriptions in gold, which must be the surnames referred to above, though one or two have *mon*. There are 50 *ashigaru*, of whom 19 have arquebuses.

BIBLIOGRAPHY

Ackroyd, Joyce, 'Women in Feudal Japan', *Transactions of the Japan Society of London*, 1957.

Asakawa, Kan'ichi, *The Documents of Iriki*, Yale University Press, 1929.

Baba, Ichiro, *Heike Monogatari Emaki*, Taiyō special edition, winter 1975, Heibonsha, Tōkyō, 1975.

Birt, Michael P., 'Warring States: A study of the Go-Hōjō daimyō and domain, 1491–1590, Ph.D. thesis, Princeton, 1983.

Birt, Michael P., 'Samurai in Passage: The Transformation of the Sixteenth Century Kantō', *Journal of Japanese Studies*, Vol. 11, No. 1, 1985.

Caron, François, *A True Description of the Mighty Kingdoms of Japan and Siam*, C.R.Boxer, London, 1935.

Inoue, Toshio, *Kenshin to Shingen: Nihon Rekishi shinshō*, Tōkyō, 1977.

Kobayashi, Keiichiro, *Kawanakajima no tatakai*, Nagano, 1985.

Kōsaka Danjō (attributed to), *Kōyō Gunkan*, in *Sengoku shiryo-shū*, series 1, Vols. 3–5.

Kuwada Tadachika (editor), *Sengoku Bushō no shōkan*, Tōkyō, 1968.

Kyūan, Rōjin, *Uma-jirushi*, Edo, 1655.

Matsumoto, Tamotsu, *Kassen Enki Emaki. Taiyō Classics and Picture Scroll Series IV*, Heibonsha, Tōkyō, 1979.

Miura Jōshin (attributed to) 'Hōjō Godaiki', in *Hōjō Shiryō-sōshō*, series 2, Vol. 1.

Nakamura, Shinju, 'Taiheiki', illustrated in *Taiyō Monthly*, 178, February 1978.

Sachiya H., and Yamamoto, S., 'Kūki to shite no Yasukuni', *Shokun*, April 1986.

Sadler, A.L., 'Heike Monogatari', *Transactions of the Asiatic Society of Japan*, Vol. 46, No. 49, Yokohama, 1918 and 1921.

Sasama, Yoshihiko, *Buke senjin sahō shūsei*, Tōkyō, 1968.

Sugiyama, Hiroshi, *Hōjō Sōun*, Odawara, 1976.

Sugiyama, Hiroshi, *Sengoku daimyō (Nihon no Rekishi 11)*, Chuo Koronsha, Tokyo, 1971.

Sugiyama, Kyushiro, 'Yasukuni no kiso chishiki jūhachi', *Shokun*, April 1986.

Takahashi, Ken'ichi, *Hata Sashimono*, Akida Shōten, Tōkyō, 1965.

Takahashi, Ken'ichi, *Daimyō-ke no kamon*, Akida Shōten, Tōkyō, 1974.

Takahashi, Ken'ichi, *Kamon, hatamoto, hachiman-ki*, Akida Shōten, Tōkyō, 1976.

Takahashi, Masato, *Buke no jirushi*, Iwasaki Bijutsusha, Tōkyō, 1979.

Turnbull, S.R., *The Samurai – A Military History*, Osprey, London, 1977, reprinted 1988.

Turnbull, S.R., *Samurai Armies 1550–1615*, Osprey, London, 1979.

Turnbull, S.R., *Warlords of Japan*, Sampson Low Library of the Past, 1979.

Turnbull, S.R., *The Mongols*, Osprey, London, 1980.

Turnbull, S.R., *The Book of the Samurai*, Arms and Armour Press, London, 1982.

Turnbull, S.R., *The Book of the Medieval Knight*, Arms and Armour Press, London, 1985.

Turnbull, S.R., *Samurai Warriors*, Blandford Press, London, 1987.

Turnbull, S.R., *Battles of the Samurai*, Arms and Armour Press, London, 1987.

Turnbull, S.R., *The Lone Samurai*, in preparation.

Turnbull, S.R., 'Shorthand of the Samurai – the Use of Heraldry in the Armies of Sixteenth Century Japan', *Proceedings of the Japan Society*, London, 1989.

Turnbull, S.R., *The Ninja*, in preparation.

Yoshida, Taiyo, *Kamon kakei jiten*, Shōbunsha, Tōkyō, 1979.

Index